# A Simple Guide to IBM SPSS® Statistics

for Versions 18.0 & 19.0

# A Simple Guide to IBM SPSS® Statistics

## for Versions 18.0 & 19.0

**Lee A. Kirkpatrick**

*The College of William & Mary*

**Brooke C. Feeney**

*Carnegie Mellon University*

WADSWORTH
CENGAGE Learning™

Australia • Brazil • Japan • Korea • Mexico • Singapore • Spain • United Kingdom • United States

## WADSWORTH
### CENGAGE Learning™

**A Simple Guide to IBM SPSS® Statistics: for Versions 18.0 & 19.0**
Lee A. Kirkpatrick, Brooke C. Feeney

Publisher: Jon-David Hague

Acquisition Editor: Timothy Matray

Editorial Assistant: Lauren Moody

Senior Media Editor: Mary Noel

Senior Marketing Manager: Jessica Egbert

Marketing Assistant: Janay Pryor

Marketing Communication Manager: Sean Foy

Manufacturing Director: Marcia Locke

Content Project Management: PreMediaGlobal

Art Director: Pamela Galbreath

Print Buyer: Rebecca Cross

Rights Acquisitions Specialist Text & Images: Don Schlotman

Cover Designer: PreMediaGlobal

Compositor: PreMediaGlobal

For product information and technology assistance, contact us at
**Cengage Learning Customer & Sales Support, 1-800-354-9706**
For permission to use material from this text or product,
submit all requests online at **www.cengage.com/permissions**
Further permissions questions can be emailed to
**permissionrequest@cengage.com**

Library of Congress Control Number: 2011928736

Student Edition:

ISBN-13: 978-1-111-35268-4

ISBN-10: 1-111-35268-2

**Wadsworth**
20 Davis Drive
Belmont, CA 94002-3098
USA

Cengage Learning is a leading provider of customized learning solutions with office locations around the globe, including Singapore, the United Kingdom, Australia, Mexico, Brazil, and Japan. Locate your local office at **www.cengage.com/global.**

Cengage Learning products are represented in Canada by Nelson Education, Ltd.

For your course and learning solutions, visit **www.cengage.com.**

Purchase any of our products at your local college store or at our preferred online store **www.cengagebrain.com**

Printed in the United States of America
1 2 3 4 5 6 7 15 14 13 12 11

# Contents

# Preface

A tremendous variety of computer software options is available for use in introductory statistics and research methods courses. Although programs designed specifically for teaching purposes and/or ease of use have obvious advantages, there are also good reasons to prefer a more advanced, research-oriented program such as SPSS. First, SPSS is in widespread use, so if one moves to another setting to finish college, pursue a graduate education, or work in an applied research setting, the odds are good that one version or another of SPSS will be available at the new location. Second, learning a powerful program such as SPSS in an introductory course prepares the student for data analysis in subsequent, more advanced courses, as well as in "real" research projects later on. It might be a little rough at first, but in the long run the extra investment of time and effort early on will pay off.

This edition, like the previous versions of this book, was written to cover what the first-time or casual user needs to know—and *only* what the user needs to know—to conduct data analyses in SPSS at the level of an introductory statistics course in psychology. Other books and manuals have been published with similar intentions, but we have not found one that we felt quite accomplished the goals as simply and inexpensively as we think should be possible. Some, for example, give equal coverage to one or more computer programs in addition to SPSS; the reader interested only in SPSS must sift through (and pay for!) the irrelevant pages to find what he or she needs. Other books attempt to achieve a level of comprehensiveness paralleling that of the program itself, delving into advanced multivariate techniques, complicated data transformation procedures, and so forth that are of little value to the beginning student. Still other books delve deeply into the theory and mathematics of the procedures, and consequently overlap with—and potentially conflict with—textbook material and classroom instruction. In contrast, our approach is to create a simple anthology of examples to illustrate the kinds of analyses typically covered in an introductory statistics course in psychology, providing just enough explanation of procedures and outputs to permit students to map this material onto their classroom and textbook knowledge.

Back in the 1990's before the Windows operating system was born, the only way to use SPSS was to learn its programming language and type in the appropriate commands. In the Windows versions, SPSS has introduced an interface (which we refer to as the *Point-and-Click Method*) that eliminates the need to learn any syntax or command language. Rather than typing commands into the program, as was required in SPSS/PC+, the user merely point-and-clicks his or her way through a series of windows and dialog boxes to specify the kind of analysis desired, the variables involved, and so forth. The program is generated internally and thus is invisible to the user. The user can then examine the output without ever viewing the program code itself—in fact, users must go out of their way to view the internally generated program code at all—and without having to ever learn any syntax or computer programming skills.

Although the simplicity of this procedure seems ideal at first, we believe it is at best a two-edged sword. IBM SPSS Statistics also permits the user to type commands the old-fashioned way (which we refer to as the *Syntax Method*) rather than simply pointing-and-clicking. There are several good reasons for learning how to use SPSS in this way rather than relying exclusively on the Point-and-Click Method. First, we think there is pedagogical value in students' learning a little computer programming, if only at the simple level of the SPSS command language, as part of an introductory statistics course. Second, for anyone planning to use SPSS for more advanced purposes than completing a few homework assignments, there is simply no escaping SPSS syntax: You'll probably want to learn it sooner or later. As you move on to more sophisticated uses of the program for real research projects, the advantages of being able to write and edit command syntax increase. For example, if you mis-specify a complex analysis and want to go back and rerun it with minor changes, or if you wish to repeat an analysis multiple times with minor variations, it is often more efficient to write and edit the program code directly than to repeat point-and-click sequences. Finally, and perhaps most important, several elements of the SPSS command language, including several procedures covered in this manual, are available only via the Syntax Method.

The question of which method is better learned first, particularly in introductory statistics courses, is a difficult one on which knowledgeable and well-intentioned instructors can (and do) honestly disagree. Consequently, the book covers both methods. Thus, beginning users and course instructors can choose to focus on one or the other method—or both, in parallel or sequentially.

In this edition, we have updated our latest book, *A Simple Guide to SPSS: For Version 17.0* (Wadsworth, 2011) to include coverage of the most recent releases from SPSS, versions 18.0 & 19.0. Users of older versions of SPSS will find one of our previous books appropriate for their respective version. Like the previous editions, this book is designed primarily to serve as an inexpensive companion volume to any standard introductory statistics text and for use in such a course. The types of analyses covered, as well as their sequence of presentation, are designed to parallel the sequence of topics covered in a typical introductory statistics course in psychology. However, the book should prove useful not only in other courses, but to first-time users of SPSS in many other contexts as well.

Good luck, and happy computing!

## About This Edition

In the last few years, the name of the program described in this book has gone through a series of changes. After many years in which it was known as *SPSS for Windows*, it briefly was renamed *PASW Statistics* ("Predictive Analytics Software") before changing again to *IBM SPSS Statistics*. The title of the current edition of this book correctly reflects the latest name. Fortunately, though, the operation and appearance of the program itself changed very little during this time—at least as far as the contents of this book are concerned—so users need not be concerned about which name appears on the version of the program they are using in conjunction with the book.

## Acknowledgments

We would like to thank the following reviewers of the manuscript for their helpful suggestions: Terry Ackerman of the University of Illinois, John Cope of East Carolina University, William Frederickson of the University of Central Oklahoma, Ira T. Kaplan of Hofstra University, Donald F. Kendrick of Middle Tennessee State University, and Michael Poteat of East Carolina University.

*Lee A. Kirkpatrick*
*Brooke C. Feeney*

## About the Authors

Lee A. Kirkpatrick is associate professor of psychology at the College of William & Mary in Williamsburg, Virginia. He received his B.S. from Lynchburg College, his M.A. in general/experimental psychology from the University of Texas at El Paso, and his Ph.D. in social/personality psychology from the University of Denver. For more information, visit his home page at http://faculty.wm.edu/lakirk.

Brooke C. Feeney is associate professor of psychology at Carnegie Mellon University. She received her B.A. from Salisbury State University, her M.A. in general/experimental psychology from the College of William & Mary, and her Ph.D. in social psychology from the State University of New York at Buffalo. Her research interests include attachment, social support, and close relationships.

# PART 1

# How to Use SPSS for Windows

SPSS for Windows, like earlier versions of SPSS, is designed to be a relatively comprehensive data analysis package for use in research and business. As such, it is designed to do a great many things. And because it does so much, there is a lot to learn in order to use it.

We have divided the book into two parts. In this first part, which all users should read, we explain the general ins and outs of using SPSS—from entering data to specifying the desired analysis to examining and manipulating output. These basic steps are a part of any kind of analysis, and users must understand them before they proceed to Part 2. Chapter 1 is a brief overview of the entire process from start to finish. Chapters 2–5 present the major steps in greater detail. In Part 2, we explain the details for conducting a variety of specific statistical procedures, by way of example. After reading Part 1, you will be ready to skip to the chapter in Part 2 that covers the specific type of analysis you want.

# Introduction to SPSS for Windows

In this chapter we provide a brief overview of the program and outline the basic procedures for (1) entering your data and naming your variables, (2) specifying statistical analyses, and (3) examining and manipulating your output. Each of these steps is then discussed in detail in Chapters 2–5.

## A Quick Tour of the Screen

The SPSS program is started in different ways depending on the installation. Typically, the program is started from Windows by simply double-clicking on the appropriate icon or by choosing it from a menu of options. After the program is finished "loading," your screen should look like Figure 1.1. If SPSS opens in a small window rather than filling the entire screen, click on the *maximize* button in the far upper-right corner to enlarge it.

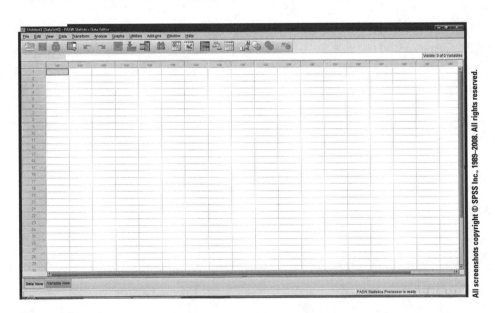

**Figure 1.1**

*Note:* Don't be surprised if when SPSS first starts up, the screen shown in Figure 1.1 is partially obscured by a small window asking "What do you want to do?" and listing several options. If this happens, choose the option "enter data" (by clicking on the little circle next to it) and then click **OK**; your screen should now look like Figure 1.1.

Let's take a quick tour of this screen. At the very top is a program title ("Untitled—SPSS Data Editor"), as well as *minimize, restore,* and *close* buttons. (If this window does not occupy the entire screen, a *maximize* button will appear instead of *restore.)*

The second line, which contains the words **File**, **Edit**, and so on, is called the *menu bar*. Clicking on any of these words produces a pull-down menu of options from which to choose in order to accomplish certain tasks. We use several of these pull-down menus in this book.

The third line, containing a row of little pictures or icons, is known as the *tool bar*. These buttons provide shortcuts for tasks otherwise accomplished via the pull-down menus. For example, the button with the little printer on it does the same thing as choosing **File**, then **Print**, from the menu bar. The particular buttons appearing on the tool bar can vary widely. The functions of these buttons are not necessarily self-evident from the little pictures, but you can find out what a particular button does by resting the cursor (using the mouse) on top of it but *not* clicking on it. When you rest the cursor on one of these buttons, a brief phrase appears summarizing the button's function. We don't use the tool bar much in this manual, but you might want to experiment with it on your own.

The remainder (and majority) of the screen is occupied by one or more windows for entering data, writing syntax, displaying output, and so forth. When you first start the program, the window in the foreground (or, alternatively, the only window visible on the screen) is the *Data Editor*.

## Using SPSS for Windows: Overview

The Data Editor is typically the starting point for everything you do in SPSS for Windows. It is a spreadsheet-style interface in which you enter your data and specify the names of your variables. Once you have done this, you proceed to the subsequent steps of specifying the analysis you want and examining your results.

### Step 1: Data Entry

The first thing you need to do, of course, is enter your data into SPSS and tell the program what these data represent. The easiest way to do this is to use the Data Editor, in which you will (1) enter the data into the rows and columns of the Data Editor, and (2) name your variables. These names will be used to specify the variables in your analyses. Chapter 2 explains these steps in detail.

Step 2: Specifying the Statistical Analysis

Once the data have been entered, the next step is to instruct SPSS to conduct the specific kind of analysis you want. There are two different ways of doing this step; each has advantages and disadvantages.

In the *Point-and-Click Method*, the desired analyses are specified by using the mouse to open menus and dialog boxes and to choose options from them. This is generally the simpler of the two methods because it does not require learning any programming language (syntax). Your computer program is, in effect, written for you, behind the scenes and out of sight, based on your choices. This method should be comfortable and familiar to experienced Windows users, as the interface is designed to be similar to most other Windows programs.

The second method, which we call the *Syntax Method*, involves using SPSS for Windows in a more "old-fashioned" way—much as the various pre-Windows versions of SPSS were used. In this method, you begin by first opening a new window, called a *Syntax Editor*, and then typing commands in the SPSS programming language that specify one or more analyses. Of course, this method requires you to learn a little of the SPSS programming language, which may sound a bit daunting at first. However, there are many advantages to learning this method, not the least of which is that (as you'll see in subsequent chapters) you can do some things in the Syntax Method that you cannot do using the Point-and-Click Method.

Chapter 3 explains the Point-and-Click Method in detail, and Chapter 4 explains the Syntax Method. In Part 2, we explain *both* ways of specifying analyses for each of the statistical procedures covered. You can use one method exclusively, or go back and forth between them whenever you wish.

Step 3: Examining and Manipulating Your Output

Once the data have been entered and the analysis has been specified using one of the two methods just described, a new window appears containing the results of your analyses. You may want to print these results and/or save them to a disk for future reference. You might also want to edit the output somewhat (for example, by deleting unneeded parts) before printing or saving. We explain how to accomplish these tasks in Chapter 5.

# Chapter 2

# Entering Data and Naming Variables

When you enter SPSS to analyze data, the first thing you need to do is type in your data and tell SPSS what the data represent. You can do this most easily using the Data Editor (as illustrated in Figure 1.1). You may want to first expand this window to fill the entire screen (by clicking the *maximize* button in the window's upper-right corner) if it doesn't already do so.

As in other spreadsheet programs, data are entered into a matrix in which *rows* represent individuals or subjects (or whatever entities were measured) and *columns* represent different variables (that is, things about those entities that have been measured). At any given moment, one particular cell of the matrix is the "currently selected" one, and is highlighted by a dark border. Initially, this is the upper-leftmost cell (that is, the intersection of row 1 and column 1), as seen in Figure 1.1. You select a new cell by using the arrow keys on the keyboard or clicking the mouse on the desired cell.

To illustrate data entry and naming variables, consider an example in which we have collected data on midterm exam scores for five students. Each student has a value on each of three variables: (1) an identification number, ranging from 1 to 5; (2) sex, coded 1 for males and 2 for females; and (3) midterm exam score. The data are as follows (note that these are the first five cases from the data in Chapter 6):

| Student | Sex | Score |
|---------|-----|-------|
| 1 | 1 | 87 |
| 2 | 1 | 53 |
| 3 | 1 | 92 |
| 4 | 1 | 70 |
| 5 | 1 | 78 |

The following two steps—entering the data and naming the variables—can be done in either order.

## Entering the Data

Entering data into the Data Editor works just as you would expect. With the upper-left cell (that is, row 1, column 1) highlighted, type the number **1** to represent the first student's identification number, and then hit the *Enter* key. As you type, a **1** appears near the top of the window; when you hit *Enter*, it appears inside the desired cell. Now use the right-arrow key to move one cell to the right (or use the mouse to click on the cell to the right), and enter **1** again, this time representing the first student's score on the second variable, sex. Next, move right again, and enter into the cell the first student's exam score of **87**. Now that the first row is completed, use the arrow keys or mouse

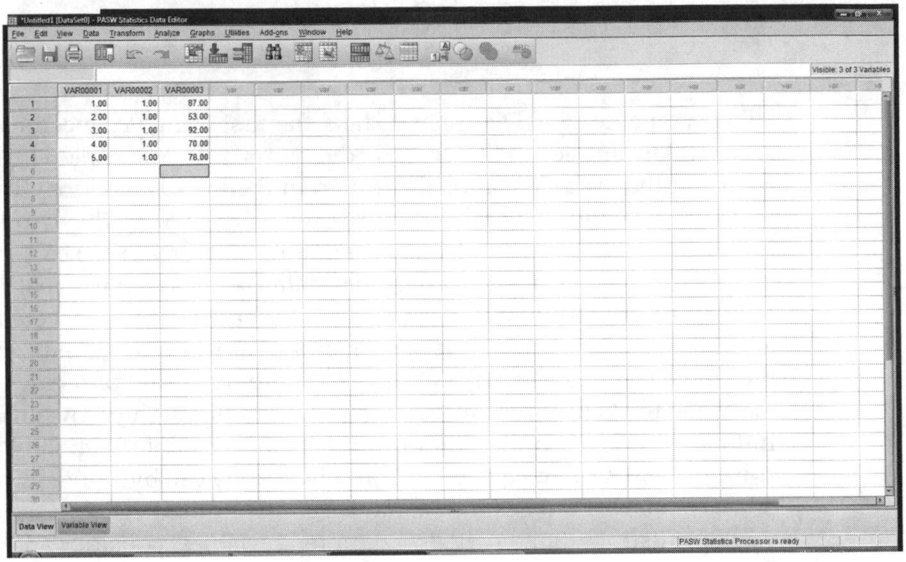

**Figure 2.1**

to move to the beginning of the second row, and enter the values for the second student in the appropriate columns. Repeat the procedure until all five rows of data have been entered. When you are finished, the screen will look like Figure 2.1.

## Types of Data

In this manual we deal only with numerical data—that is, data composed solely of numbers. For various reasons, even categorical variables such as sex (male, female) or group assignment in an experiment (for example, control vs. experimental) are best "coded" (entered) as numbers rather than as letters or words. The most obvious system for coding categories of a variable is simply to assign the numbers 1, 2, 3, and so on to the categories. For the variable *sex* in our example, we assigned the value 1 to men and 2 to women. Of course, this assignment is arbitrary, and we might just as well have done it the other way around. The important thing is that you remember which is which.

If your data contain decimals, just type the decimal point where appropriate using a period. You may enter as many or as few decimal places as necessary.

**Figure 2.2**

## Naming the Variables

Whenever you enter data into SPSS, you need to decide what names to assign to your variables and tell SPSS what these names are so you can refer to them later in specifying the analyses you want. Use words or abbreviations that will help you to remember what the variables are. For example, *gender* or *sex* is obviously a good name for a variable that distinguishes men from women. It really makes no difference to SPSS, though, and as far as SPSS is concerned, you could just as well call this variable *cabbage* or *acijd5*. This won't bother SPSS in the least, but it is likely to confuse *you* at some point and should probably be avoided. The important thing is that you assign each of your variables a distinct name and that you remember what these names represent.

In earlier versions of SPSS for Windows (prior to version 12.0), variable names were restricted to no more than 8 characters in length. Although much longer names are now permitted, we still recommend using short, simple variable names for most purposes, as we have done throughout this book.

In our example there are three columns of data representing the students' identification number, sex, and exam score. First, click on the tab labeled "Variable View" in the lower-left corner of the screen (see Figure 2.1). This will reveal a new screen that looks like Figure 2.2. In this screen, each variable is represented by a row containing various bits of information about it. For our current purposes, we wish only to change the names of the variables.

In the first column of the table, you can see that your first variable is named "VAR00001"; this is the name SPSS assigns to the variable by default. This is okay as long as you are able to remember what it represents, but a better idea is to name the variable something more meaningful and easier to remember. To do so, simply click on **VAR00001,** and edit the contents of this box so it contains the name you wish to assign to the variable. The easiest way to do this is to press the *Backspace* key, which deletes the contents of the box, and then type in the variable name you prefer—in this case, "student."

Now use the arrow keys or mouse to move down to the second row to change "VAR0002" to "sex," and then to the third row to change "VAR00003" to "score." Finally, click on the "Data View" tab in the lower-left corner of the screen to return to the screen containing the actual data values.

Once the data have been entered and variables named, it is a good idea to save your work. See Appendix A for details on how to do this.

# Chapter 3

# Specifying Analyses Using the Point-and-Click Method

Once the data have been entered into the Data Editor, you're ready to tell SPSS what you would like it to do with those data—that is, what kind of statistical analysis you wish to conduct. In Part 2 of this manual we explain exactly how to do this, using both the Point-and-Click Method and the Syntax Method, for a variety of statistical procedures. In this short chapter we briefly preview the Point-and-Click Method; in Chapter 4 we preview the Syntax Method.

To specify analyses using the Point-and-Click Method, you usually begin by clicking on **Analyze** on the menu bar, which produces a pull-down menu listing various categories of statistical procedures from which to choose. Choosing any of these options by clicking on it produces yet another menu of options. For example, clicking on **Compare Means** on the **Analyze** menu produces a list of options, including **One-Sample T Test . . .** and **One-Way ANOVA . . .** , as illustrated in Figure 3.1. (As will be the case for most illustrations in this book, some of the details may differ slightly, depending on your particular installation.) Finally, clicking on one of *these* options produces a

**Figure 3.1**

dialog box in which you specify the details for the analysis you have selected. In this box you specify such things as the names of the variables to be used in the analysis, details concerning the manner in which the analysis is to be conducted, and choices concerning what information is to be included in the output. In Part 2 we explain the details for different kinds of analyses. Once you have made all your choices, click on a button labeled **OK** and SPSS will spring into action. That's all there is to it.

Although we have described the Point-and-Click and Syntax Methods as mutually exclusive alternatives, a kind of "hybrid" method is also available. After specifying an analysis using the Point-and-Click Method, you can click on a button labeled **Paste** rather than the one labeled **OK**. This tells SPSS to show you the command (syntax) corresponding to the analysis you just specified by pointing-and-clicking—that is, what you would have to type in order to use the Syntax Method. This command is "pasted" into the Syntax Editor, where you can examine it and then run it as if you had typed it in yourself (see Chapter 4). This "hybrid" method can be very helpful in learning how to write SPSS command language.

If you plan to use the Point-and-Click Method exclusively, you can skip the next chapter and proceed to Chapter 5 on viewing and manipulating output. However, we recommend going ahead and learning the Syntax Method, too. As you will see in several chapters in Part 2, for some kinds of analyses the Syntax Method is simpler, or makes it possible to do things that cannot be done with the Point-and-Click Method. It will be worthwhile in the long run to become familiar with both methods.

# Chapter 4

# Specifying Analyses Using the Syntax Method

To use the Syntax Method, you need a *Syntax Editor* in which to type and edit SPSS program commands ("syntax") to specify the desired analysis. To open the syntax editor, (1) click on **File** on the menu bar, then (2) click on **New** in the resulting pull-down menu, and finally (3) click on **Syntax** in the resulting submenu. The Syntax Editor now appears in the foreground. You may expand it to fill the screen by using the *maximize* button.

At this point, the Syntax Editor window is blank, and a cursor appears in its upper-left corner. If you begin typing, what you type will appear in the window at the point where the cursor is located. As you'll see, this window operates very much like a (very simple) word-processing program, and you can use the *Delete* (or *DEL*) key, the *Insert* (or *INS*) key, the *Backspace* key, and so forth to edit your commands and correct your errors. In the Syntax Method sections of the chapters in Part 2, we explain exactly what to type into this window to specify the desired analysis. Figure 4.1 illustrates the syntax window after a command (from Chapter 6) has been typed in.

The narrow window on the left side of the screen is designed to serve as a table of contents for your syntax, and SPSS will automatically add items to this section as you type commands in the main window. Also, you will notice that as you type commands, the text might suddenly change color and little drop-down menus might sometimes pop up. SPSS is just trying to help you type the correct commands, a feature which you may feel free to ignore or use as you wish.

## Executing ("Running") the Analysis

Once your commands have been typed into the Syntax Editor, you need to tell SPSS to "execute" or "run" them—that is, to actually carry out the instructions you have written. First, make sure that the cursor is located somewhere—anywhere—on the command you want to execute by using the mouse and clicking somewhere on the command. Now locate the *Run* button on the tool bar near the top of the screen. It is the button with a right-pointing arrow on it. You can see it in Figure 4.1 under the word **Graphs**. Click on this button and SPSS will leap into action.

If you typed more than one command into the Syntax Editor, you can execute several commands at once by first highlighting the commands you wish to run. To do this, (1) use the mouse to position the cursor just to the left of the first command, and (2) click (*but do not release!*) the left mouse button; (3) while continuing to hold this button down, use the mouse to reposition the cursor to the end of the last command to be executed; and

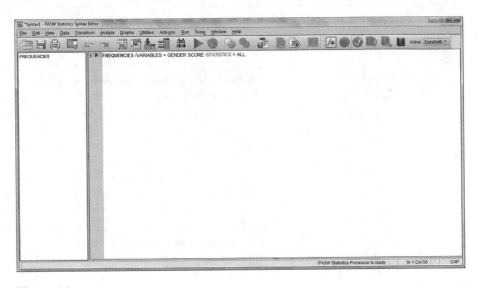

**Figure 4.1**

(4) release the mouse button. In Windows jargon, this is referred to as "clicking-and-dragging." Then click on the *Run* button to execute the highlighted commands.

Yet another option is available as well. The Syntax Editor has an extra item on its menu bar labeled with the word **Run**. Click on **Run**, and a pull-down menu presents you with several options, including **All** (which runs all the commands appearing in the Syntax Editor without your having to highlight them), **Selection** (which runs only the commands highlighted as just described), and **To End** (which runs all commands beginning at cursor).

## Some General Notes on SPSS Commands

If you follow our examples carefully and don't improvise too much, you shouldn't have too many problems. However, a few general features of SPSS commands are worth knowing:

1. All SPSS commands should begin in the first column (that is, don't indent them) and must end with a period (.). If you ever get an error message (see the following section), the first thing to check is whether you left out a period at the end of a command. No matter what the error message, a

missing period may very well be the culprit. This is an easy mistake to make and, believe us, we both do it all the time.

2. Between the beginning of the command and the final period, there is considerable flexibility in format. For example, wherever a space is required (between words, for example), you can always use two or more spaces if you prefer. In addition, commas and spaces are usually interchangeable.

3. If a command is too long to fit on one line, just hit *Enter* at some point to move to the next line and continue typing the command. Use as many lines as you need: SPSS will just keep reading until it finds a period (don't forget that period!) signaling the end of the command. These continuation lines do not have to begin in the first column; in fact, we personally prefer to indent continuation lines a few spaces to make the program look nice and enhance readability.

4. As you will see, many SPSS commands include one or more subcommands that specify details of the analysis. Subcommands are usually separated from each other with slashes (/). (Note that these are forward slashes, not backslashes.) Because subcommands are part of the same command, it doesn't matter if you put extra spaces between them, or if you begin subcommands on a new line, or whatever. Again, though, we sometimes like to start a new (indented) line for each subcommand for aesthetic purposes, but this is by no means necessary.

## Errors

One of the drawbacks of using the Syntax Method is that you can easily make mistakes in entering data or specifying SPSS commands. This doesn't happen in the Point-and-Click Method, because SPSS writes your commands for you (behind the scenes) based on the choices you specify in menus and dialog boxes—and it knows what it's doing.

Because mistakes are easy to make, when you execute commands from the Syntax Editor, the analysis may not run. As usual, however, SPSS will put the output window in the foreground so you can see your results; in this case, your results will include *error messages*. These are clearly identifiable; they generally say "Error:" or "Warning:" followed by some (usually cryptic) message intended to help you identify the problem. Explaining all these messages is far beyond the scope of this manual, but if you've followed our examples and instructions carefully, the only kinds of errors you're likely to encounter will involve typographical errors, missing periods at the ends of commands, and so forth. After reading (and trying to decipher) the error messages, get the Syntax Editor back into the foreground (click on **Window** on the menu bar and choose **Syntax1 - SPSS Statistics Syntax Editor** from the resulting menu), and try to figure out what you did wrong. After making any necessary repairs, run the command(s) again as just described.

Once you have written your syntax and confirmed that it works, it is a good idea to save your work. See Appendix A for details on how to do this.

# Chapter 5

# Viewing and Manipulating Output

When you run an analysis using either the Syntax Method or the Point-and-Click Method, your output appears in a new kind of window called the *Output Viewer*. This window contains SPSS's report on the results of your analysis, and might look something like Figure 5.1. (This particular screen resulted from the sample problem in Chapter 6.) On the left side of the screen is an outline or table of contents listing the sections of your output; to the right (and taking up most of the screen) is the output itself.

*Note:* Depending on your installation, you may see some extra text at the top of your output that does not appear in our illustration. For example, if you used the Syntax Method, the SPSS commands you typed into the Syntax Editor might be reprinted at the beginning of the output. Also, if you used the Syntax Method to enter your data, the beginning of the output might include a few lines of text containing information about the format in which

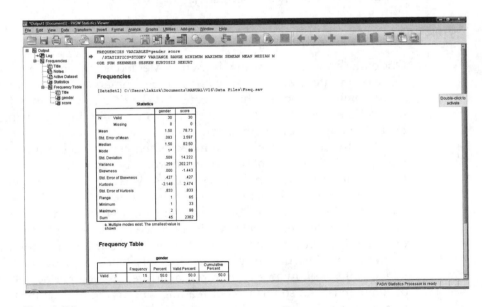

**Figure 5.1**

the data were read by SPSS. In Figure 5.1, such information would have appeared in the right side of the screen above the title "Frequencies."

## Viewing Output

Obviously, the first thing you want to do is examine the results. You can move around within the window using the arrow keys on the keyboard, or use the mouse to manipulate the scroll bars along the window's right and bottom edges. For a different view, try clicking on **File** on the menu bar at the top of the screen, then click on **Print Preview** on the pull-down menu. This gives you a full-screen view of an entire page of output, just as it would appear if you printed it. Experiment with the **Zoom In** and **Zoom Out** buttons on this new screen to change the view to a size you like, and with the **Next Page** and **Prev Page** buttons if the output comprises more than one page. Scroll bars appear on the right and/or bottom edges of the screen when you need them. To return to the main Output Viewer screen (Figure 5.1) at any time, click on **Close**.

## Editing Output

Before saving and/or printing the output file, you might want to modify it somewhat. Editing the contents of the Output Viewer window seems very complicated to us, so for beginning users we recommend not doing much editing of output files.

The one editing task that is relatively simple, and often desirable, is deleting sections of unwanted output. In many procedures, SPSS prints out tables of information you don't really need, so you might want to delete these sections to save paper and unclutter your printout. This is where the outline on the left side of the Output Viewer window comes into play. If you click on an item in that outline—say, **Title** or **Statistics**—two things happen: (1) the word you clicked on is selected (and appears highlighted) and (2) the specified section of the output appears in the large window (if it didn't already) surrounded by a box identifying what is in that section. You can delete this entire section by simply hitting the *Delete* key on the keyboard.

## Printing Output

Printing the contents of the output window is simple. From the main Output Viewer window (Figure 5.1), click on **File** on the menu bar and choose **Print** from the pull-down menu. A dialog box appears somewhere on your screen. First, be sure the box labeled "Copies" contains the number of copies you want printed (usually **1**). Then choose between "All visible output" and "Selection" by clicking on the circle to the immediate left of the one you choose.

"All visible output" means to print everything displayed in the output window: This is probably the one you want. If you want to print only part of the output, we recommend editing the output in SPSS (see the preceding section) to remove the unwanted portions, and then printing "All visible output." You can also print from the **Print Preview** window by simply clicking on the **Print** button at the top of this screen, and then following the instructions just given.

## Saving Output

It is usually a good idea to save your output for future reference, particularly if you don't print out a hard copy. See Appendix A for details on how to do this.

Once you have finished examining, saving, and/or printing your output, you may wish to return to another window to run more procedures, modify your data, and so on. Just click on the *minimize* button in the upper-right corner of the screen, or click on **Window** on the menu bar and choose the window to which you wish to return.

As with the rest of SPSS for Windows, it should be obvious that many other options and features are available in the Output Viewer to control the display, editing, and printing of the output, but they are beyond the scope of this manual. Once you feel comfortable with the basics of SPSS, you might want to explore some of these fancier features on your own.

## Exiting SPSS for Windows

Once you are finished analyzing your data, reviewing your output, and so forth, you'll be ready to exit SPSS for Windows. This can be done in various ways. One way is to choose **File** from the menu bar and then **Exit** from the pull-down menu; another is to click the *close* button in the very upper-right corner of the screen (the button with the ⊠ on it). If you haven't saved your work, you will be prompted about whether you wish to save the contents of each of the windows (data, output, and perhaps syntax) that are currently open. If you have already saved these items before exiting, as we suggested (and as detailed in Appendix A), there is no need to do so again. If you forgot to save something, you can click on **Cancel** when asked about saving one of these files, then go back to the appropriate window and save it properly before exiting.

# PART 2

# Procedures

The preceding chapters provided an overview of the various steps involved in conducting data analysis in SPSS, from data entry to output. In Part 2, we fill in the details for a variety of common statistical procedures, showing how to conduct each analysis using both the Point-and-Click Method and the Syntax Method. For each type of analysis, we present a sample problem, show how to conduct the analysis using each of the two methods, and then explain the output produced by the procedure.

In most cases, the two methods produce exactly the same results. However, in some cases, certain useful options are available in the Syntax Method that are not available in the Point-and-Click Method. In some of these cases, extra steps are required in the Point-and-Click Method to obtain comparable results. The format of the output differs somewhat depending on which method you used, but they should be sufficiently similar that you should have no trouble understanding your output if it looks a bit different from ours.

# Chapter 6

# Frequency Distributions and Descriptive Statistics

## Sample Problem

Fifteen men and fifteen women in an introductory psychological statistics course have taken their midterm exams. Their scores are listed here. (For gender, 1 = male and 2 = female.)

| Student | Gender | Score | Student | Gender | Score |
|---------|--------|-------|---------|--------|-------|
| 1 | 1 | 87 | 16 | 2 | 89 |
| 2 | 1 | 53 | 17 | 2 | 73 |
| 3 | 1 | 92 | 18 | 2 | 91 |
| 4 | 1 | 70 | 19 | 2 | 76 |
| 5 | 1 | 78 | 20 | 2 | 75 |
| 6 | 1 | 73 | 21 | 2 | 89 |
| 7 | 1 | 91 | 22 | 2 | 81 |
| 8 | 1 | 60 | 23 | 2 | 83 |
| 9 | 1 | 77 | 24 | 2 | 68 |
| 10 | 1 | 82 | 25 | 2 | 86 |
| 11 | 1 | 85 | 26 | 2 | 55 |
| 12 | 1 | 33 | 27 | 2 | 89 |
| 13 | 1 | 88 | 28 | 2 | 89 |
| 14 | 1 | 98 | 29 | 2 | 70 |
| 15 | 1 | 88 | 30 | 2 | 93 |

In this problem we wish to construct frequency distributions and obtain some basic descriptive statistics for the variables *gender* and *score*. Refer back to Figure 2.1 (page 6) to see what the screen will look like after you have entered the first five lines of these data.

## Analysis

Following the procedure outlined in Chapter 2, enter the data into the first three columns of the Data Editor and label the variables **Student**, **Gender**, and **Score**.

### Point-and-Click Method

To begin, click on **Analyze** on the menu bar. This produces a pull-down menu containing a variety of options, such as **Compare Means**, **Correlate**, and so on. Now click on **Descriptive Statistics**. This produces yet another

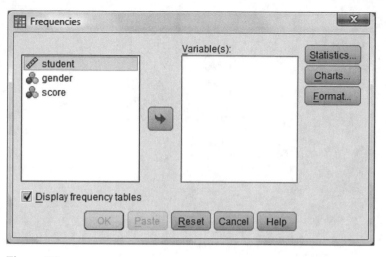

**Figure 6.1**

menu containing items such as **Frequencies . . .** , **Descriptives . . .** , and **Explore . . . .** Choose **Frequencies . . .** to specify that you want frequency distributions. This produces a dialog box somewhere on your screen, on top of the other windows, that looks like Figure 6.1.

Many of the dialog boxes for specifying procedures in SPSS for Windows are similar to this dialog box in several respects. On the left is a box containing the names of all your variables. To the right is another (empty) box labeled "Variable(s)." The goal is to move from the left box to the right box the names of the variable(s) for which you want frequency distributions. Do this by clicking on one of the variable names to highlight it, and then clicking on the right-arrow button between the boxes to move it. The variable name disappears from the left box and appears in the right box. (Alternatively, you can just double-click on the variable name and it will move to the other box immediately.) Simply repeat this procedure for each variable desired. If you make a mistake or change your mind, you can single-click on a variable in the right-hand box, and then click on the middle arrow (which will have switched to a left-pointing arrow when you clicked on the variable name) to remove it from the "Variable(s)" list. In this example, we want to choose **Gender** and **Score**, the two variables of interest. You may now click on **OK** to run the analysis. However, if you would like to have SPSS print out descriptive statistics or graphs in addition to the frequency distribution, do not click on **OK** but instead keep reading.

*Descriptive Statistics.*    At the bottom of this dialog box, you'll see three other buttons labeled **Statistics . . .** , **Charts . . .** , and **Format. . . .** If you wish to

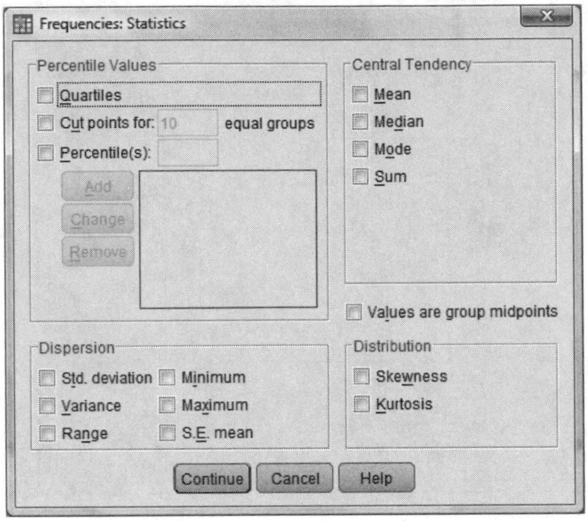

**Figure 6.2**

obtain descriptive statistics along with your frequency table, click on **Statis-tics . . .** to produce a new dialog box, as illustrated in Figure 6.2.

Apart from the section labeled "Percentile Values" and the line "Values are group midpoints," the remaining sections of the box list a variety of descriptive statistics. Simply click on the little box to the left of each statistic you wish SPSS to calculate for you; a check mark will appear in each se-lected box. (Note that if you wish to unselect a box you've already selected, simply click on it again.) The sample output shown in the next main section, titled Output, is the result of requesting all available statistics by checking all six boxes under "Dispersion," all four boxes under "Central Tendency," and both boxes under "Distribution." The box next to "Values are group midpoints" does not need to be selected, however. When finished, click on **Continue** to return to the previous dialog box (Figure 6.1). Click on **OK** to run the analysis, or follow the instructions in the next section to obtain a graphical frequency distribution in the form of a histogram or bar graph as well.

*Histograms and Bar Graphs.*    To obtain histograms and/or bar charts in ad-dition to frequency tables (and in addition to or instead of descriptive statis-tics), click on **Charts . . .** at the right in the dialog box illustrated in Figure 6.1 to produce a new dialog box (not illustrated). Initially, SPSS assumes you do not want any graphs ("charts")—the little circle next to "None" is selected by default. Click on the circle next to "Bar chart" or "Histogram" to indicate the kind of frequency distribution graph you prefer. Then click **Continue** to return to the previous dialog box (Figure 6.1), and click on **OK** to run the analysis.

Syntax Method

Open the Syntax Editor as described in Chapter 4. Type the following command (don't forget the period at the end!) in this window and then click on the *Run* button to execute the analysis:

```
FREQUENCIES /VARIABLES = GENDER SCORE /STATISTICS = ALL.
```

This command tells SPSS to produce frequency distributions. The subcommand **/VARIABLES** specifies the variables for which you would like SPSS to produce a frequency distribution, in this case **GENDER** and **SCORE**. Note that variable names are separated by spaces or commas. Alternatively, you can write **/VARIABLES = ALL**, replacing the list of variable names with the word **ALL**. This tells SPSS to create a frequency distribution for every variable it knows about.

*Descriptive Statistics.* The subcommand **/STATISTICS = ALL** tells SPSS to produce all available summary statistics for the variables listed on the **/VARIABLES** subcommand. If you want only certain statistics, you need to consult a more detailed manual to determine how to replace **ALL** with names of specific statistics. (The more common ones are **MEAN**, **MEDIAN**, **STDDEV**, and **VARIANCE**.) However, it's usually easier to just ask for **ALL** statistics and then ignore the ones you don't care about. If you do not want any descriptive statistics, simply leave off the **/STATISTICS** subcommand entirely.

*Histograms and Bar Graphs.* To obtain histograms in addition to the tabular frequency distribution, simply add a **/HISTOGRAM** subcommand to the **FREQUENCIES** command, either in addition to or instead of a **/STATISTICS** subcommand. To request a histogram for the variable **SCORE**, for example, use this command:

```
FREQUENCIES /VARIABLES = SCORE /HISTOGRAM.
```

If you wish to produce a bar chart instead of a histogram, replace the subcommand **/HISTOGRAM** with the subcommand **/BARCHART**.

## Output

The output produced by SPSS for the sample problem is illustrated in Figure 6.3.

# Frequencies

**Statistics**

|  |  | gender | score |
|---|---|---|---|
| N | Valid | 30 | 30 |
|  | Missing | 0 | 0 |
| Mean |  | 1.50 | 78.73 |
| Std. Error of Mean |  | .093 | 2.597 |
| Median |  | 1.50 | 82.50 |
| Mode |  | 1ª | 89 |
| Std. Deviation |  | .509 | 14.222 |
| Variance |  | .259 | 202.271 |
| Skewness |  | .000 | -1.443 |
| Std. Error of Skewness |  | .427 | .427 |
| Kurtosis |  | -2.148 | 2.474 |
| Std. Error of Kurtosis |  | .833 | .833 |
| Range |  | 1 | 65 |
| Minimum |  | 1 | 33 |
| Maximum |  | 2 | 98 |
| Sum |  | 45 | 2362 |

a. Multiple modes exist. The smallest value is shown

## Frequency Table

**gender**

|  |  | Frequency | Percent | Valid Percent | Cumulative Percent |
|---|---|---|---|---|---|
| Valid | 1 | 15 | 50.0 | 50.0 | 50.0 |
|  | 2 | 15 | 50.0 | 50.0 | 100.0 |
|  | Total | 30 | 100.0 | 100.0 |  |

**Figure 6.3**

For each variable, SPSS produces a frequency distribution and a set of descriptive statistics; we have included only the frequency table for the variable *gender* here due to space considerations. The table of statistics should be self-explanatory. The first column in each Frequency Table lists all values that were found on the variable; the second column ("Frequency") lists

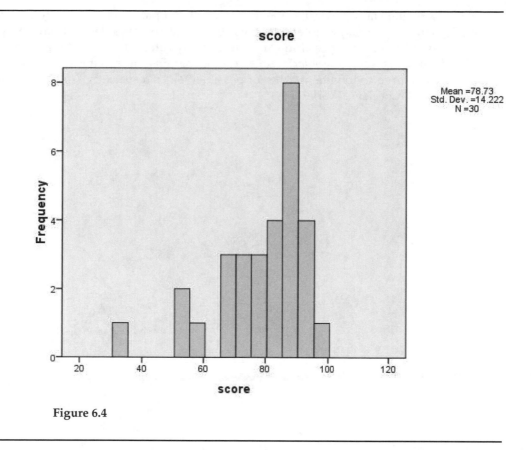

**Figure 6.4**

the number of cases having that value; the third column ("Percent") is the percentage of all cases having this value (that is, frequency divided by total number of cases); the fourth column ("Valid Percent") is the percentage of all "valid" cases—that is, cases that were not missing data on this variable—having that value; and the fifth column lists the cumulative percentage for that value—that is, the percentage of valid cases having that value or less. Note that "Percent" and "Valid Percent" will be identical if there are no missing values on this variable.

*Histograms and Bar Graphs.*    Figure 6.4 illustrates a histogram for the variable *score*, as produced by the procedure described earlier. Notice that SPSS has divided the range of scores into 5-point intervals (e.g., 30–35, 35–40, and so on), and the heights of the respective bars represent the frequencies of these categories rather than of individual scores. Had you asked SPSS for a *bar chart* instead of a *histogram*, SPSS would not have grouped the scores into intervals like this; instead, each individual value would have its own separate bar representing the frequency of that particular score. For this reason, it is generally preferable to use bar charts for variables that have only a small number of possible values (especially categorical or "nominal-level" variables, such as *gender*), and to use histograms for variables that can take on a large or infinite number of possible values (especially "interval-level" and "ratio-level" variables).

# Chapter 7

# One-Sample *t*-Test

## Sample Problem

The superintendent of the Riverwalk school district claims that the students in his district are more intelligent, on the average, than the general population of students. The mean IQ of the general population of school children is 105. A study was conducted to determine the IQs of a sample of school children in the Riverwalk district. The results are as follows:

| Student | IQ Score | Student | IQ Score |
|---------|----------|---------|----------|
| 1  | 110 | 16 | 110 |
| 2  | 105 | 17 | 117 |
| 3  | 102 | 18 | 98  |
| 4  | 112 | 19 | 124 |
| 5  | 120 | 20 | 107 |
| 6  | 107 | 21 | 112 |
| 7  | 99  | 22 | 122 |
| 8  | 100 | 23 | 104 |
| 9  | 109 | 24 | 105 |
| 10 | 103 | 25 | 110 |
| 11 | 115 | 26 | 120 |
| 12 | 125 | 27 | 125 |
| 13 | 115 | 28 | 120 |
| 14 | 106 | 29 | 100 |
| 15 | 110 | 30 | 110 |

In this problem, we are testing the null hypothesis that the mean IQ of all school children in the Riverwalk school district equals 105. This will be assessed by examining a random sample of Riverwalk students. This value was selected because it was already known that 105 is the overall mean IQ of all students in all school districts. We want to know whether the Riverwalk population is any different. Is the mean of this sample significantly different from 105?

## Analysis

Following the procedure outlined in Chapter 2, enter the data into the first two columns of the Data Editor and label the variables **student** and **iq**.

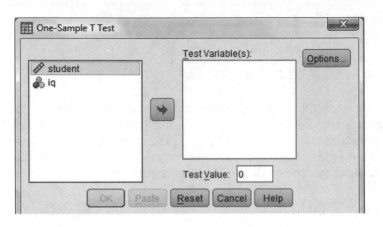

**Figure 7.1**

Point-and-Click Method

Click on **Analyze** on the menu bar, and then choose **Compare Means**. From the resulting menu (which was illustrated in Figure 3.1), choose **One-Sample T Test . . . .** This produces a dialog box that looks like Figure 7.1.

In the left-hand box, click on **iq,** then click on the right-arrow button between the boxes to move **iq** to the box labeled "Test Variable(s)." Next, click in the box labeled "Test Value" and edit its contents (which appear as **0** initially) so it reads **105**. This is the null hypothesis value against which you are testing the sample mean. (Of course, you would just leave this box as **0** if you wanted to test the hypothesis that the mean IQ equals zero.) Now click on **OK** and the analysis will run.

Syntax Method

Open the Syntax Editor, type the following command (don't forget the period at the end!), and click on the *Run* button to execute the analysis:

**T-TEST TESTVAL = 105 /VARIABLES = IQ.**

The syntax for this command, as you can see, is quite simple. The meaning of the command **T-TEST**, which is also used in the next two chapters, is self-evident. The subcommand **TESTVAL =** specifies the null hypothesis value to be tested; in this case, the value of interest is 105. The **/VARIABLES** subcommand then specifies the variables to be tested. In this case, we want to know only if the mean of the variable **IQ** is significantly different from 105. If we had several variables, and we wanted to test the mean of each (separately) against the null hypothesis value of 105, we would list the other variable names after **IQ**, separated by spaces or commas.

## Output

The output produced by SPSS for the sample problem is shown in Figure 7.2.

SPSS first prints some descriptive statistics for the variable *iq*, including number of cases, mean, standard deviation, and standard error. Beneath the descriptive statistics are the results of the significance test. "Mean Difference" is the difference between the observed sample mean (110.73) and the hypothesized mean (105). SPSS also prints out a 95% confidence interval for the difference between means, which in this case goes from 2.73 to 8.74.

Is a mean difference of 5.733 large enough to be significantly different from 105? The results of the *t*-test show that $t = 3.900$, with 29 ($N - 1$) degrees of freedom ("df"). The two-tailed *p*-value for this result is .001 (rounded off to three decimal places). The result is considered statistically significant if the *p*-value is less than the chosen alpha level (usually .05 or .01). In this case, *p* is definitely less than .05 (and .01), so the result is considered statistically significant and the null hypothesis is rejected.

## T-Test

**One-Sample Statistics**

|     | N | Mean | Std. Deviation | Std. Error Mean |
|-----|-----|--------|------------------|-------------------|
| iq  | 30  | 110.73 | 8.051            | 1.470             |

**One-Sample Test**

|     | Test Value = 105 | | | | | |
|-----|------|------|----------------|-----------------|---------------------------------|---------------------------------|
|     |      |      |                | Mean            | 95% Confidence Interval of the Difference | |
|     | t    | df   | Sig. (2-tailed) | Difference      | Lower | Upper |
| iq  | 3.900 | 29  | .001           | 5.733           | 2.73  | 8.74  |

**Figure 7.2**

If you were doing the problem by hand, you would use a table in your statistics textbook to determine the critical *t*-value associated with 29 degrees of freedom—this value is 2.045 (for alpha = .05)—and then compare the observed *t*-value to the critical value. In this case, the observed *t* of 3.90 is greater than the critical value, so again you would have rejected the null hypothesis.

Note that the output from most statistical procedures in SPSS works this same way. That is, SPSS prints the *p*-value associated with the test statistic, and it is up to you to decide whether *p* is sufficiently small to reject the null hypothesis (that is, whether *p* is smaller than your chosen alpha level of .05, .01, or whatever). Both methods—comparing critical versus observed *t*-values and comparing critical (alpha) versus observed (*p*) probabilities—lead to the exact same conclusion for any given problem.

# Chapter 8

# Independent-Samples *t*-Test

## Sample Problem

The psychology department at Rockhaven University conducted a study to determine the effectiveness of an integrated statistics/experimental methods course as opposed to the traditional method of taking the two courses separately. It was hypothesized that the students taking the integrated course would conduct better quality (more controlled and statistically sound) research projects than students in the traditional courses as a result of their integrated training. To determine whether there actually was a difference in student performance as a result of integrated versus traditional training, the final research projects of 20 students from an integrated course and 20 students from a traditional course were evaluated. Their scores are listed here. (For condition, 1 = integrated course and 2 = traditional course.)

| Student | Condition | Score | | Student | Condition | Score |
|---------|-----------|-------|---|---------|-----------|-------|
| 1 | 1 | 87 | | 21 | 2 | 82 |
| 2 | 1 | 95 | | 22 | 2 | 72 |
| 3 | 1 | 89 | | 23 | 2 | 95 |
| 4 | 1 | 74 | | 24 | 2 | 60 |
| 5 | 1 | 73 | | 25 | 2 | 90 |
| 6 | 1 | 92 | | 26 | 2 | 87 |
| 7 | 1 | 63 | | 27 | 2 | 89 |
| 8 | 1 | 90 | | 28 | 2 | 86 |
| 9 | 1 | 94 | | 29 | 2 | 76 |
| 10 | 1 | 84 | | 30 | 2 | 74 |
| 11 | 1 | 91 | | 31 | 2 | 85 |
| 12 | 1 | 90 | | 32 | 2 | 75 |
| 13 | 1 | 75 | | 33 | 2 | 90 |
| 14 | 1 | 93 | | 34 | 2 | 91 |
| 15 | 1 | 87 | | 35 | 2 | 88 |
| 16 | 1 | 85 | | 36 | 2 | 63 |
| 17 | 1 | 90 | | 37 | 2 | 70 |
| 18 | 1 | 89 | | 38 | 2 | 72 |
| 19 | 1 | 87 | | 39 | 2 | 84 |
| 20 | 1 | 85 | | 40 | 2 | 60 |

In this problem, we are testing the null hypothesis that there is no difference in student performance as a result of the integrated versus traditional courses; that is, the mean difference between the conditions in the population from which the sample was drawn is zero. The alternative hypothesis reflects the psychology department's belief that the population means for the two groups of students are not equal (that is, the belief that course format had some kind of effect on quality of research projects).

## Analysis

Following the procedure outlined in Chapter 2, enter the data into the first three columns of the Data Editor and label the variables **student**, **cond**, and **score**.

### Point-and-Click Method

Click on **Analyze** on the menu bar, and then choose **Compare Means**. From the resulting menu, choose **Independent-Samples T Test . . . .** This produces a dialog box that looks like Figure 8.1.

In this dialog box, your list of variables appears in the box to the left, and you must (1) move one (or more) of the variables into the box labeled "Test Variable(s)" to select your dependent variable(s) and (2) move *one* of your variables into the box labeled "Grouping Variable" to identify the groups to be compared (that is, to select the independent variable). First, click on **score** (the dependent variable in our example) in the left-hand box to select it; then click on the upper right-arrow button pointing to the "Test Variable(s)" box; **score** disappears from the left-hand box and reappears under "Test Variable(s)." Next, click on **cond** (the independent variable in

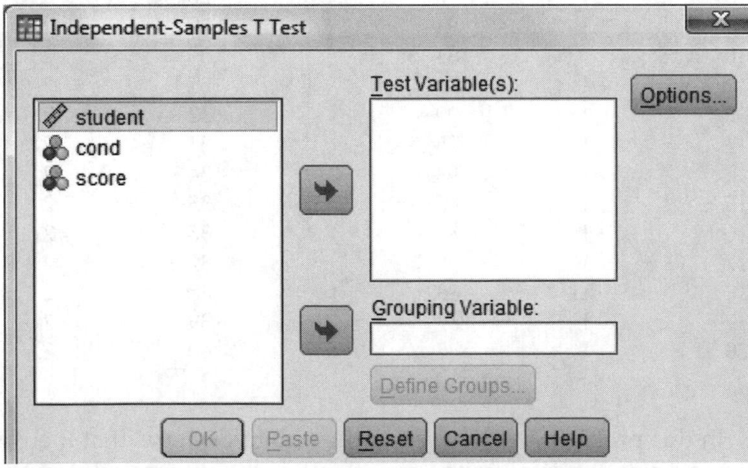

**Figure 8.1**

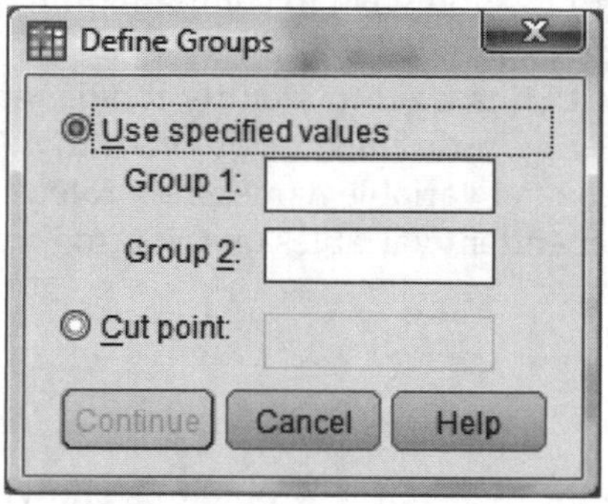

**Figure 8.2**

our example) to select it, and then click on the right-arrow button pointing to the "Grouping Variable" box to move it there. The name **cond** now appears under "Grouping Variable," followed by a set of parentheses containing two question marks. This is to call your attention to the fact that one additional specification is required before you can execute this analysis.

When you selected **cond** as your grouping variable, something else happened on your screen as well. The button labeled **Define Groups . . .** suddenly looked different. Whereas it previously appeared fuzzy and with lightly colored lettering, it now appears sharp and distinct. This is because the button was not functional until you selected the grouping variable—but it is now functional and quite important. Click on it and another dialog box appears (see Figure 8.2) in which you must specify the two values of **cond** that represent the two groups you wish to compare. In our case, **cond** was coded simply as **1** (integrated course) and **2** (traditional course). Click in the box next to "Group 1" and, when the cursor appears there, type the number **1**. Then use the mouse to click in the box next to "Group 2" and type the number **2**. Now click on **Continue** to return to the dialog box illustrated in Figure 8.1. In this box, click on **OK** to run the analysis.

Syntax Method

Open the Syntax Editor, type the following command (don't forget the period at the end!), and then click on the *Run* button to execute the analysis:

`T-TEST /GROUPS = COND (1,2) /VARIABLES = SCORE.`

To use the **T-TEST** command in SPSS to test a hypothesis about the equality of means of two independent populations, the subcommand **/GROUPS** is used to name the independent variable whose values identify the two groups being compared (in this problem, **COND**). After the independent variable name, you must type, in parentheses, the two values of this variable that identify the two groups you wish to compare (in this problem, **1** and **2**). The two values must be separated by a comma.

The subcommand **/VARIABLES** is used to identify the dependent variable(s) (in this problem, **SCORE**) whose means you wish to compare between groups. You can specify several variable names, separated by commas or spaces, to specify multiple dependent variables on the same command.

## Output

The output produced by SPSS for the sample problem is shown in Figure 8.3.

SPSS first prints the number of cases, means, standard deviations, and standard errors on the dependent variable separately for each group. In this case, the two groups are defined by the variable *cond* (1 = integrated; 2 = traditional).

"Levene's Test for Equality of Variances" is provided next by SPSS. This test is probably not of interest to most readers. (It represents a test of the hypothesis that the populations from which the groups were sampled have equal variances.)

Beneath (or to the right of) Levene's Test are the results of the "*t*-test for Equality of Means." The information provided in the row labeled "Equal variances not assumed" reports the results of a *t*-test that is sometimes used when there is reason to believe that the two population variances are not equal. SPSS reports the observed *t*-value, the degrees of freedom ("df"), and the two-tailed *p*-value ("Sig. (2-tailed)"). This test is not often discussed in introductory statistics courses, so if you haven't discussed the test in class, just ignore this part of the output. Also reported on this line are the difference between the means, standard error of the difference, and the 95% confidence interval for the difference between population means.

The most commonly used test is the one listed in the row labeled "Equal variances assumed." Because we are assuming that the two population variances are equal, a pooled variance estimate is used to combine the two sample variances to obtain the most accurate estimate of the variance common to both populations.

The observed *t*-value for this problem is 2.043, with degrees of freedom (total sample size minus 2) equal to 38. The two-tailed probability of .048 is less than .05 and, therefore, the test is considered significant (though barely) at the .05 level.

To verify this, you can use your statistics textbook to determine the critical *t*-value associated with 38 degrees of freedom: critical $t_{.05}(38) =$ approximately 2.03. The observed *t*-value (2.04) is greater (barely) than the critical *t*-value; therefore, the null hypothesis is rejected at the .05 level of significance.

# T-Test

## Group Statistics

| | cond | N | Mean | Std. Deviation | Std. Error Mean |
|---|---|---|---|---|---|
| score | 1 | 20 | 85.65 | 8.242 | 1.843 |
| | 2 | 20 | 79.45 | 10.782 | 2.411 |

## Independent Samples Test

| | | Levene's Test for Equality of Variances | | t-test for Equality of Means | | | | | 95% Confidence Interval of the Difference | |
|---|---|---|---|---|---|---|---|---|---|---|
| | | F | Sig. | t | df | Sig. (2-tailed) | Mean Difference | Std. Error Difference | Lower | Upper |
| score | Equal variances assumed | 3.880 | .056 | 2.043 | 38 | .048 | 6.200 | 3.035 | .057 | 12.343 |
| | Equal variances not assumed | | | 2.043 | 35.551 | .049 | 6.200 | 3.035 | .043 | 12.357 |

Figure 8.3

# Chapter 9

# Dependent-Samples (Matched-Pairs, Paired Samples) *t*-Test

## Sample Problem

An investigator believes (based on past research) that parents who use positive verbal statements (polite requests and suggestions) have children who are more socially accepted and more positive in interactions with peers. Although children acquire behavioral information from sources other than parents (TV, peers, and so on), more induction (coaching children by introducing consequences for behaviors and supplying rationales that support them) on the part of parents, as opposed to more power-assertive and permissive types of discipline, facilitates a prosocial behavioral orientation in children that leads to greater social competence and greater acceptance by peers. Twenty first-grade children (who were rated by teachers and peers as aggressive) and their parents were selected for a study to determine whether a seminar instructing on inductive parenting techniques improves social competency in children. The parents attended the seminar for one month. The children were tested for social competency before the course began and were retested six months after the completion of the course. The results of the social competency test are shown here (with higher scores indicating greater social competency):

| Child | Pre | Post | Child | Pre | Post |
|-------|-----|------|-------|-----|------|
| 1 | 31 | 34 | 11 | 31 | 28 |
| 2 | 26 | 25 | 12 | 27 | 32 |
| 3 | 32 | 38 | 13 | 25 | 25 |
| 4 | 38 | 36 | 14 | 28 | 30 |
| 5 | 29 | 29 | 15 | 32 | 41 |
| 6 | 34 | 41 | 16 | 27 | 37 |
| 7 | 24 | 26 | 17 | 37 | 39 |
| 8 | 35 | 42 | 18 | 29 | 33 |
| 9 | 30 | 36 | 19 | 31 | 40 |
| 10 | 36 | 44 | 20 | 27 | 28 |

In this problem, we are testing the null hypothesis that there is no difference between the means of pre- and postseminar social competency scores. In other words, the parenting seminar has no effect on child social competency scores; or, stated yet another way, the population mean of difference scores (preseminar minus postseminar scores, or vice versa) equals zero. The alternative hypothesis reflects the investigator's belief that there is a difference between pairs of pre- and postseminar scores; the population mean of difference scores does not equal zero (that is, the seminar has some effect on social competency scores).

## Analysis

Following the procedure outlined in Chapter 2, enter the data into the first three columns of the Data Editor and label the variables **child**, **pre**, and **post**.

Point-and-Click Method

Click on **Analyze** on the menu bar, and then choose **Compare Means**. From the resulting menu (which was illustrated in Figure 3.1), choose **Paired-Samples T Test** . . . . This produces a dialog box that looks like Figure 9.1.

In this dialog box, your list of variables appears in the box in the upper left, and you identify as follows the ones whose means you want to compare. First, click on **pre**, then on the arrow key between the boxes; this will move the first variable over to the box on the right. Then click on **post,** then the arrow, to move the second variable. (Alternatively, if you hold down the *Shift* key while clicking on **pre** and then **post,** they will both be highlighted; clicking on the arrow next will move them both together.) If you make a mistake, just click on the variable name in the right-hand box, and the arrow will switch to point in the other direction. Clicking on it then will move the variable back to the list on the left.

When SPSS computes difference scores, it computes the first variable ("variable 1") minus the second variable ("variable 2"). In this example, the difference scores will be computed as **pre** minus **post.** This can be confusing, as positive differences will mean that scores decreased from pretest to posttest, and negative differences will mean they increased. To avoid this confusion, you can move the variables to the right-hand box in the opposite order, so that differences are computed as **post** minus **pre.** In either case, the significance test tests the hypothesis that in the population, the mean of these difference scores equals zero. Now click on **OK** to execute the analysis.

**Figure 9.1**

### Syntax Method

Open the Syntax Editor, type the following command (don't forget the period at the end!), and then click on the *Run* button to execute the analysis:

```
T-TEST /PAIRS = PRE POST.
```

As usual, the **T-TEST** command in SPSS is used to test the null hypothesis that two population means are equal.

The **/PAIRS** subcommand tells SPSS that you wish to conduct a paired *t*-test to test whether the means of two variables are equal. After the **/PAIRS** subcommand, you must specify the names of the two variables whose means you wish to compare, separated by a space or comma. Difference scores will be computed by subtracting the first variable minus the second—in this case, **pre** minus **post**—so choose the order you prefer.

## Output

The output produced by SPSS for the sample problem is shown in Figure 9.2.

SPSS first produces some descriptive statistics (number of pairs, mean, standard deviation, and standard error) for each variable (in this case, *pre* and *post*). In addition, SPSS also calculates the correlation coefficient between the two variables *pre* and *post*, and the two-tailed probability for a test of the null hypothesis that the population correlation coefficient equals zero. These results appear under "Correlation" and "Sig" in the middle section of the output. This test is probably not of interest to you at this point. A more direct way of calculating correlation coefficients is presented in Chapter 14.

A paired *t*-test is calculated by first computing a set of difference scores in which one variable is subtracted from the other. The mean of these difference scores is given under "Paired Differences" and is equivalent to the difference between the mean of *pre* and the mean of *post*. The standard deviation and standard error of these difference scores are listed next, followed by the 95% confidence interval for the population mean of difference (*pre – post*) scores.

Finally, the results of the *t*-test itself are presented. The observed *t*-value, calculated as the mean difference (–3.750) divided by its standard error (.876), is –4.280. The degrees of freedom (number of pairs of observations minus 1) and the two-tailed *p*-value are also printed. Note that although the computed *p*-value for this problem is reported as ".000," this does not mean that it is actually equal to zero. SPSS rounds off *p*-values (in this case, to three decimal places). Therefore, any *p*-value less than .0005 is printed as .000.

To check this, you can use your statistics textbook to determine the critical *t*-value associated with 19 degrees of freedom and an alpha level of .001 (this is the smallest level of significance listed in most textbook tables) for a two-tailed test: critical $t_{.001}(19) = 3.883$. The observed *t*-value is greater than the critical *t*-value; therefore, the null hypothesis is rejected at the .001 level of significance.

# T-Test

**Paired Samples Statistics**

| | | Mean | N | Std. Deviation | Std. Error Mean |
|---|---|---|---|---|---|
| Pair 1 | pre | 30.45 | 20 | 4.019 | .899 |
| | post | 34.20 | 20 | 6.066 | 1.356 |

**Paired Samples Correlations**

| | | N | Correlation | Sig. |
|---|---|---|---|---|
| Pair 1 | pre & post | 20 | .771 | .000 |

**Paired Samples Test**

| | | Paired Differences | | | | | | | |
|---|---|---|---|---|---|---|---|---|---|
| | | | | | 95% Confidence Interval of the Difference | | | | |
| | | Mean | Std. Deviation | Std. Error Mean | Lower | Upper | t | df | Sig. (2-tailed) |
| Pair 1 | pre - post | -3.750 | 3.919 | .876 | -5.584 | -1.916 | -4.280 | 19 | .000 |

Figure 9.2

# Chapter 10

# One-Way Between-Groups (Independent Groups) ANOVA

## Sample Problem

Sleep researchers have postulated that, in a broad evolutionary sense, sleeping more poorly during periods of perceived environmental threat may have survival value. Previous research has indicated that individuals experiencing anxiety or stress exhibit reduced periods of deep sleep and increased periods of light sleep (because one can most easily be aroused by a sound in the environment while in light sleep). An attachment researcher conducted a study to examine the effects of anxious, avoidant, and secure attachment styles on the physiology of sleep. The investigator hypothesized that children with anxious (and perhaps avoidant) attachment styles experience more sleep disturbances than children with secure attachment styles because they feel responsible for monitoring the external environment and regulating the distance between themselves and their caregivers. These children may find it difficult to sleep when their caregivers are physically absent and may develop patterns of light sleep because of the need to be aware of the caregiver's presence at all times. Deep sleep can be experienced as threatening to the attachment bond and thus dangerous to the child. The sleep patterns of 10 secure, 10 anxious, and 10 avoidant 5-year-old children were monitored. Of primary importance to the attachment researcher was the overall percentage of time that each child spent in deep (delta) sleep. It was hypothesized that children who are insecurely attached to their primary caregivers will spend a lower percentage of time in deep (delta) sleep as compared to their secure counterparts. Following is the average amount of time that each child spent in delta sleep, expressed as a percentage of total sleep time. (For the attachment styles, 1 = secure, 2 = anxious, and 3 = avoidant.)

| Subject | Attachment Style | Delta Sleep | Subject | Attachment Style | Delta Sleep |
|---|---|---|---|---|---|
| 1 | 1 | 21 | 11 | 2 | 17 |
| 2 | 1 | 21 | 12 | 2 | 17 |
| 3 | 1 | 25 | 13 | 2 | 15 |
| 4 | 1 | 23 | 14 | 2 | 15 |
| 5 | 1 | 24 | 15 | 2 | 15 |
| 6 | 1 | 23 | 16 | 2 | 14 |
| 7 | 1 | 23 | 17 | 2 | 20 |
| 8 | 1 | 22 | 18 | 2 | 13 |
| 9 | 1 | 22 | 19 | 2 | 14 |
| 10 | 1 | 22 | 20 | 2 | 19 |

| Subject | Attachment Style | Delta Sleep | Subject | Attachment Style | Delta Sleep |
|---------|------------------|-------------|---------|------------------|-------------|
| 21 | 3 | 18 | 26 | 3 | 17 |
| 22 | 3 | 20 | 27 | 3 | 15 |
| 23 | 3 | 18 | 28 | 3 | 16 |
| 24 | 3 | 19 | 29 | 3 | 17 |
| 25 | 3 | 17 | 30 | 3 | 18 |

In this problem, we are testing the null hypothesis that, on average, the three populations of children (secure, anxious, and avoidant attachment styles) spend an equal percentage of time in deep (delta) sleep:

$H_0$: 

| Mean delta for the population of secure children | = | Mean delta for the population of anxious children | = | Mean delta for the population of avoidant children |
|---|---|---|---|---|

The test of this hypothesis, sometimes referred to as the "omnibus" null hypothesis, is conducted as an *F*-test.

## Post-Hoc Test

Rejection of the "omnibus" null hypothesis in ANOVA tells us only that not all population means are equal. It does not indicate which attachment groups are significantly different from which others. One way to further examine group differences is to use *post-hoc* or *a posteriori* multiple comparison tests, such as the Student-Newman-Keuls or Tukey HSD test. In our example, we use Tukey HSD tests to test for differences between all possible pairs of means.

## Planned Comparisons/Contrasts

Another approach to multiple comparisons in ANOVA is to test more specific hypotheses, which have been specified in advance, about which means differ from which other means or which combinations of means differ from other combinations of means. These tests are known as *planned comparisons, contrasts,* or *a priori* multiple comparison tests.

In our example, we test two contrasts. For each contrast, we are testing a different null hypothesis. First, we want to test the null hypothesis that the mean percentage of time spent in delta sleep for the population of secure children is equal to the mean of the means of the populations of anxious and avoidant children. Mathematically,

$$H_0: \text{Mean delta for the population of secure children} = \frac{\text{Mean delta for the population of anxious children} + \text{Mean delta for the population of avoidant children}}{2}$$

The appropriate contrast coefficients for this problem are **–2** for the secure group (attstyle = 1), **1** for the anxious group (attstyle = 2), and **1** for the avoidant group (attstyle = 3). Note that we could just as easily have reversed all the signs and used the coefficients 2, –1, and –1, respectively.

For the second contrast, we want to test the null hypothesis that the mean percentage of time spent in delta sleep for the population of anxious children is equal to the mean percentage of time spent in delta sleep for the population of avoidant children:

$$H_0: \quad \begin{array}{c} \text{Mean delta for the} \\ \text{population of} \\ \text{anxious children} \end{array} \quad = \quad \begin{array}{c} \text{Mean delta for the} \\ \text{population of} \\ \text{avoidant children} \end{array}$$

The appropriate coefficients for attstyles 1 through 3, respectively, are 0, 1, and –1.

In this example, we are testing only two contrasts, and they happen to be orthogonal. However, it is not necessary for contrasts specified in SPSS to be orthogonal, and there is no limit on the number you may specify in a given analysis.

## Analysis

Following the procedure outlined in Chapter 2, enter the data into the first three columns of the Data Editor and label the variables **subject**, **attstyle**, and **delta**.

### Point-and-Click Method

Click on **Analyze** on the menu bar, and then choose **Compare Means**. From the resulting menu, choose **One-Way ANOVA . . . .** This produces a dialog box that looks like Figure 10.1.

This dialog box is very similar to that for the independent-samples *t*-test, as discussed in Chapter 8. In this dialog box, your list of variables appears in the box to the left, and you must (1) move one (or more) of your variables into the box labeled "Dependent List" to select your dependent variable(s) and (2) move *one* of your variables into the box labeled "Factor" to identify the groups to be compared (that is, to select the independent variable). First, click on **delta** (the dependent variable in our example) in the left-hand box to select it; then click on the upper right-arrow pointing to the "Dependent List" box; **delta** disappears from the left-hand box and reappears under "Dependent List." Next, click on **attstyle** (the independent variable in our example) to select it, and then click on the right-arrow button pointing to the "Factor" box to move it there. The name **attstyle** now appears under "Factor."

If you wish to have SPSS print out means and other descriptive statistics along with the results of the *F*-test—and, of course, you do!—there is still one more step. In the dialog box illustrated in Figure 10.1, click on **Options . . .** to bring up another dialog box. In this box, which is illustrated in Figure 10.2,

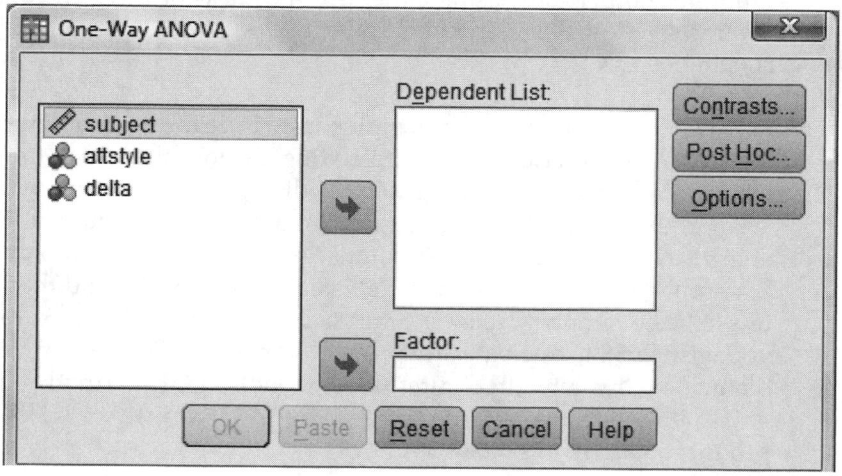

**Figure 10.1**

click on the box under "Statistics," next to "Descriptive." Then click on
**Continue** to return to the previous dialog box.

If you wish to conduct only the "omnibus" analysis of variance to test
the hypothesis that all three population means are equal, you are done. Click

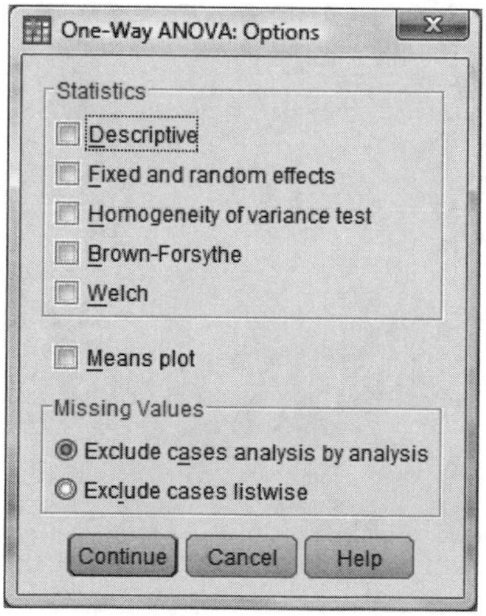

**Figure 10.2**

on **OK** to execute the analysis. If, in addition, you wish to conduct tests of multiple comparisons, using either post-hoc tests or planned comparisons/contrasts, follow the instructions in the corresponding sections below before clicking on **OK**.

*Post-Hoc Tests.*    To conduct post-hoc tests in SPSS, specify your variables, and so on, as described in the preceding section; then click on the button labeled **Post Hoc . . .** at the right in the dialog box illustrated in Figure 10.1. This produces a new dialog box (see Figure 10.3) containing a list of available tests. For simple pairwise comparisons, the most commonly used tests are probably Student-Newman-Keuls (labeled "S-N-K") and the Tukey HSD test (labeled simply "Tukey"). Simply click on the box(es) next to the test(s) you wish SPSS to calculate and print. Then click on **Continue** to return to the dialog box illustrated in Figure 10.1, and click on **OK** to run the analysis.

To illustrate, the output produced by specifying Tukey's HSD test is reproduced later in this chapter.

*Planned Comparisons/Contrasts.*    To conduct tests of planned comparisons or contrasts, specify your variables, and so on, as described previously, and then click on the button labeled **Contrasts . . .** at the right in the dialog box illustrated in Figure 10.1. This produces a new dialog box as illustrated in Figure 10.4.

**Figure 10.3**

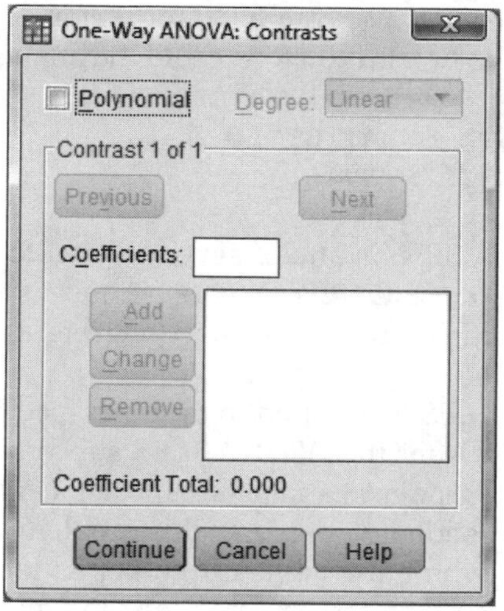

**Figure 10.4**

Specifying your contrast coefficients in this window can be a little tricky, but experiment a little and you'll get the hang of it. For the first contrast in our example, we wish to use the coefficients –2, 1, and 1, in that order, for *attstyle* groups 1, 2, and 3. To specify these coefficients, click in the box to the right of "Coefficients" and type the number of the coefficient for the first (lowest-numbered) group, in this case **–2**. Now click on the button labeled **Add** to add this coefficient to your list of coefficients (which is displayed in the box to the right of the **Add** button). Now click in the "Coefficients" box again, and type the coefficient for the second group (in this example, type **1**), and then click again on **Add**. Finally, click on the "Coefficients" box again, type **1** (the last coefficient), and click on **Add**. Your list of three coefficients now appears in the box to the right of the **Add** button: –2, 1, and 1, from top to bottom. If this is the only contrast you wish to test, click on **Continue** to return to the main One-Way ANOVA dialog box (Figure 10.1), and then click on **OK** to run the analysis.

In this example, however, we wish to test a second contrast as well. After specifying the coefficients for the first contrast as just described, click on **Next** to the right of the phrase "Contrast 1 of 1." This phrase now changes to "Contrast 2 of 2," which is what you specify now. The box containing your previously entered coefficients is again blank. Repeat the procedure outlined above to enter the coefficients **0, 1,** and **–1** in order. Once these have been entered, click on **Continue** to return to the main One-Way ANOVA dialog box, and then click on **OK** to run the analysis.

Syntax Method

Open the Syntax Editor, type the following command (don't forget the period at the end!), and then click on the *Run* button to execute the analysis:

```
ONEWAY /VARIABLES = DELTA BY ATTSTYLE
       /STATISTICS = DESCRIPTIVES.
```

The **ONEWAY** command in SPSS is one of several ways to conduct a one-way analysis of variance. We use **ONEWAY** here because it has several useful subcommands for conducting multiple comparison tests, as illustrated in later sections.

The subcommand **/VARIABLES** is required in order to specify the variables to be used in the analysis. After the **/VARIABLES** subcommand, you must type the name(s) of the dependent variable(s) whose means you wish to test for each level of the independent variable. In this problem, the dependent variable is **DELTA**. After typing the name of the dependent variable, you must type the word **BY**, then type the name of your independent variable. In this problem, the independent variable is **ATTSTYLE**.

The **/STATISTICS = DESCRIPTIVES** subcommand tells SPSS to provide, in addition to the *F*-test itself, descriptive statistics (including the sample size, mean, standard deviation, standard error, and 95% confidence limits for the mean, minimum, and maximum values) for each group.

*Post-Hoc Tests.*   In our example, we have chosen to use Tukey HSD tests for pairwise comparisons among group means. To specify this, the **ONEWAY** command is modified as follows:

```
ONEWAY /VARIABLES = DELTA BY ATTSTYLE
       /STATISTICS = DESCRIPTIVES
       /RANGES = TUKEY.
```

In general, to request a test of multiple comparisons, simply add a **/RANGES** subcommand to the end of your **ONEWAY** command line, in addition to the **/STATISTICS**. (Notice that the command is now too long to fit on a single line, so we have finished it on a second line. We indented the second line for purely aesthetic reasons; this was not necessary.) This subcommand tells SPSS to conduct multiple comparison tests for all possible differences among the group means. In this example, we have selected the Tukey HSD test. Some other commonly used options include:

```
/RANGES = DUNCAN (for Duncan multiple range test)
/RANGES = SNK (for Student-Newman-Keuls test)
/RANGES = SCHEFFE (for Scheffé's test)
/RANGES = LSD (for Least Significant Difference test).
```

*Planned Comparisons/Contrasts.* To conduct tests of contrasts, you specify the coefficients for your groups by using the subcommand **/CONTRAST**. After each **/CONTRAST** subcommand, simply type the desired contrast coefficients, in order, for the lowest- to highest-numbered groups. You can type as many **/CONTRAST** subcommands as you wish on a given **ONEWAY** command.

```
ONEWAY /VARIABLES DELTA BY ATTSTYLE
       /CONTRAST -2 1 1
       /CONTRAST 0 1 -1.
```

The **ONEWAY /VARIABLES DELTA BY ATTSTYLE** command line is identical to that used in the previous example.

## Output

The output produced by SPSS for the omnibus analysis is shown in Figure 10.5.

After some descriptive statistics, the ANOVA results are printed. Three sources of variability are listed: "Between Groups" (variability due to the treatment effect: differences between groups as a result of attachment style), "Within Groups" (variability reflecting random error), and "Total." For each, SPSS reports the sum of squares, degrees of freedom, and mean square (sum of squares divided by degrees of freedom).

### Oneway

**Descriptives**

delta

| | N | Mean | Std. Deviation | Std. Error | 95% Confidence Interval for Mean | | Minimum | Maximum |
|---|---|---|---|---|---|---|---|---|
| | | | | | Lower Bound | Upper Bound | | |
| 1 | 10 | 22.60 | 1.265 | .400 | 21.70 | 23.50 | 21 | 25 |
| 2 | 10 | 15.90 | 2.283 | .722 | 14.27 | 17.53 | 13 | 20 |
| 3 | 10 | 17.50 | 1.434 | .453 | 16.47 | 18.53 | 15 | 20 |
| Total | 30 | 18.67 | 3.346 | .611 | 17.42 | 19.92 | 13 | 25 |

**ANOVA**

delta

| | Sum of Squares | df | Mean Square | F | Sig. |
|---|---|---|---|---|---|
| Between Groups | 244.867 | 2 | 122.433 | 41.425 | .000 |
| Within Groups | 79.800 | 27 | 2.956 | | |
| Total | 324.667 | 29 | | | |

**Figure 10.5**

The *F* ratio, calculated as the mean square between divided by the mean square within, is listed next in the table. The *F* ratio in this example equals 41.425, and its associated *p*-value ("Sig.") is reported as .000. (As in previous examples, this does not mean that *p* is exactly equal to zero, but rather that the probability is less than .0005 and has been rounded off to .000.) Thus we reject the null hypothesis and conclude that the three attachment styles differ with respect to the mean amount of time that children spend in deep (delta) sleep.

Post-Hoc Tests

SPSS prints out the results of the Tukey HSD tests in two different ways, as shown in Figure 10.6.

Each of the six rows of the upper table represents a comparison of two groups; for example, the first row compares Group 1 vs. Group 2. Actually, each comparison appears twice because the comparison of 1 vs. 2 (first row) is for all practical purposes the same as the comparison of 2 vs. 1 (third row). In any case, for each pairwise comparison of interest, SPSS prints out the difference between the means (for example, 6.700 or –6.700 for Group 1 vs. Group 2), along with a standard error, *p*-value ("Sig."), and confidence interval. In this example, Groups 1 and 2 are significantly different from each other (*p* is listed as .000, meaning it is less than .0005 and rounded off) and Groups 1 and 3 are significantly different from each other (again, *p* is reported as .000). However, Groups 2 and 3 do not differ from each other (*p* = .113).

The second part of the output presents this information in a different (and we think confusing) way, by identifying *homogeneous subsets* of means— that is, by showing sets of means that do not differ significantly from each other. In the left column, the groups are listed in order from that with the smallest mean (Group 2 in this case) to that with the largest mean (Group 1 in this case). To the right are two columns listing the actual means, grouped into two subsets: Subset 1 contains Groups 2 (mean = 15.90) and 3 (mean = 17.50), whereas subset 2 contains only Group 1 (mean = 22.60). This indicates that Groups 2 and 3 form a homogeneous subset whose means are not significantly different from one another. Group 1, however, is in a different subset, indicating that its mean *does* differ significantly from the means of the groups in subset 1. That is, the means of the "anxious" (Group 2) and "avoidant" (Group 3) groups are not significantly different from each other, but each is significantly different from the mean of the "secure" group (Group 1).

Planned Comparisons/Contrasts

When contrasts or planned comparisons are requested, the output shown in Figure 10.7 is produced by SPSS in addition to the ANOVA results previously illustrated.

SPSS produces a matrix of contrast coefficients (a reminder about which groups were assigned which coefficients for each test), followed by the significance tests for each contrast. Two different significance tests are provided

## Post Hoc Tests

**Multiple Comparisons**

Dependent Variable: delta
Tukey HSD

| (I) attstyle | (J) attstyle | Mean Difference (I-J) | Std. Error | Sig. | 95% Confidence Interval Lower Bound | 95% Confidence Interval Upper Bound |
|---|---|---|---|---|---|---|
| 1 | 2 | 6.700* | .769 | .000 | 4.79 | 8.61 |
|   | 3 | 5.100* | .769 | .000 | 3.19 | 7.01 |
| 2 | 1 | -6.700* | .769 | .000 | -8.61 | -4.79 |
|   | 3 | -1.600 | .769 | .113 | -3.51 | .31 |
| 3 | 1 | -5.100* | .769 | .000 | -7.01 | -3.19 |
|   | 2 | 1.600 | .769 | .113 | -.31 | 3.51 |

*. The mean difference is significant at the .050 level.

## Homogeneous Subsets

**delta**

Tukey HSD[a]

| attstyle | N | Subset for alpha = .050 — 1 | Subset for alpha = .050 — 2 |
|---|---|---|---|
| 2 | 10 | 15.90 | |
| 3 | 10 | 17.50 | |
| 1 | 10 | | 22.60 |
| Sig. | | .113 | 1.000 |

Means for groups in homogeneous subsets are displayed.
  a. Uses Harmonic Mean Sample Size = 10.000.

**Figure 10.6**

for each contrast, labeled as "Assume equal variances" and "Does not assume equal variances," respectively. The more commonly used test is the one listed under "Assume equal variances." In this test, the error term for every contrast is based on the $MS_{within}$ from the omnibus ANOVA.

For each contrast, SPSS prints: (1) the value of the contrast itself, a linear combination of the contrast coefficients and sample means (labeled "Value of Contrast" in the output); (2) a standard error; (3) the observed $t$ statistic; (4) the error degrees of freedom for the test; and (5) a two-tailed probability or $p$-value. In this example, the first contrast, which compares Group 1 with Groups 2 and 3 combined, is significant: $t = -8.861$ with 27 degrees of freedom, $p = .000$ (that is, $p$ is less than .0005). The second contrast (Group 2 vs. Group 3) is also significant, with $t = -2.081$ and $p = .047$.

**Contrast Coefficients**

| | attstyle | | |
|---|---|---|---|
| Contrast | 1 | 2 | 3 |
| 1 | -2 | 1 | 1 |
| 2 | 0 | 1 | -1 |

**Contrast Tests**

| | | Contrast | Value of Contrast | Std. Error | t | df | Sig. (2-tailed) |
|---|---|---|---|---|---|---|---|
| delta | Assume equal variances | 1 | -11.80 | 1.332 | -8.861 | 27 | .000 |
| | | 2 | -1.60 | .769 | -2.081 | 27 | .047 |
| | Does not assume equal variances | 1 | -11.80 | 1.169 | -10.094 | 23.237 | .000 |
| | | 2 | -1.60 | .852 | -1.877 | 15.144 | .080 |

**Figure 10.7**

Some formulas for calculating significance tests for contrasts by hand employ *F*-tests rather than *t*-tests. The *t*-tests computed by SPSS produce identical results to these tests: For each contrast, just square the observed *t*-value produced by SPSS to find the corresponding *F*-value.

# Chapter 11

# Two-Way Between-Groups (Independent Groups) ANOVA

## Sample Problem

A male psychology student has been interested all year in dating one of his female colleagues; however, he has been uncertain about how to approach her and introduce himself. He knows that first impressions are very important, and he feels that the way he presents himself initially will determine the course of their relationship. Because he is a psychology student and is familiar with research methodology, he decides to conduct a study to determine the effectiveness of various approaches to meeting someone. The three approaches he wants to investigate are as follows: (1) casual conversation approach (engaging in casual conversation with the subject, saying whatever comes naturally); (2) humor approach (using humor to break the ice and generate interest on the part of the subject); and (3) pick-up line approach (using a clever pick-up line to express interest and generate interest on the part of the subject). The researcher also feels that his attractiveness may have an impact on the effectiveness of each approach; therefore, he decides to include attractiveness as a second independent variable. To help him conduct the study, he recruits two male friends who have pleasant, friendly personalities like his own. One of these friends has been consistently rated by a random sample of females as attractive, and the other has been consistently rated as unattractive. The study is conducted with a random selection of 30 female students who are sitting alone in the student union lounge. The attractive confederate accosts five subjects using the casual conversation approach, five subjects using the humor approach, and five subjects using the pick-up line approach. The unattractive confederate also accosts different sets of five students for each approach. The measure of success for each approach is the length of time (in minutes) the confederates are able to engage each subject in conversation. The results are as follows (for attractiveness, 1 = attractive and 2 = unattractive; for approach, 1 = conversation, 2 = humor, and 3 = pick-up line):

| Subject | Attractiveness | Approach | Time |
|---------|----------------|----------|------|
| 1 | 1 | 1 | 43 |
| 2 | 1 | 1 | 35 |
| 3 | 1 | 1 | 52 |
| 4 | 1 | 1 | 48 |
| 5 | 1 | 1 | 30 |
| 6 | 1 | 2 | 61 |
| 7 | 1 | 2 | 45 |

| Subject | Attractiveness | Approach | Time |
|---------|----------------|----------|------|
| 8 | 1 | 2 | 52 |
| 9 | 1 | 2 | 39 |
| 10 | 1 | 2 | 43 |
| 11 | 1 | 3 | 1 |
| 12 | 1 | 3 | 2 |
| 13 | 1 | 3 | 3 |
| 14 | 1 | 3 | 2 |
| 15 | 1 | 3 | 4 |
| 16 | 2 | 1 | 15 |
| 17 | 2 | 1 | 22 |
| 18 | 2 | 1 | 10 |
| 19 | 2 | 1 | 27 |
| 20 | 2 | 1 | 20 |
| 21 | 2 | 2 | 60 |
| 22 | 2 | 2 | 42 |
| 23 | 2 | 2 | 53 |
| 24 | 2 | 2 | 40 |
| 25 | 2 | 2 | 39 |
| 26 | 2 | 3 | 2 |
| 27 | 2 | 3 | 3 |
| 28 | 2 | 3 | 1 |
| 29 | 2 | 3 | 1 |
| 30 | 2 | 3 | 4 |

A two-way ANOVA will test three null hypotheses corresponding to (1) the main effect of attractiveness, (2) the main effect of approach type, and (3) the interaction of attractiveness and approach type.

## Analysis

Following the procedure outlined in Chapter 2, enter the data into the first four columns of the Data Editor and label the variables **subject**, **attract**, **approach**, and **time**.

In our example, the number of subjects in each of the six groups is the same ($n = 5$). When these $n$'s are unequal, however, matters can become complicated: Several methods are available for computing sums of squares and $F$-tests, each of which may produce different results for the main effects. In this chapter we describe only the most widely accepted method for these circumstances—the so-called *Type III sums of squares* or *regression approach*, which (fortunately) is the default method used by SPSS for Windows. When $n$'s are equal, as in the present example, these methods produce identical results and you need not be concerned with these issues.

Moreover, when $n$'s are unequal, there are two different ways of computing the *marginal means* corresponding to the main effects—that is, the overall means for estimating the effects of each independent variable, averaging across the other independent variable. With unequal *n*'s, most experts recommend computing so-called *unweighted* marginal means (rather than *weighted* marginal means) for examining the main effects. Although an explanation of the issues involved is well beyond the scope of this manual, we explain how to obtain both kinds of marginal means.

Point-and-Click Method

Click on **Analyze** on the menu bar. Next, choose **General Linear Model** from the pull-down menu, and then choose **Univariate**. This produces a dialog box that looks like Figure 11.1.

This dialog box is very similar to that for the independent-samples *t*-test and the one-way ANOVA, as discussed in Chapters 8 and 10. In this dialog box, your list of variables appears in the box to the left, and you must (1) move one of the variables into the box labeled "Dependent Variable" to select your dependent variable and (2) move one or more (in this example, two) of your variables into the box labeled "Fixed Factor(s)" to identify the independent variable(s).

**Figure 11.1**

First, click on **time** (the dependent variable in our example) in the left-hand box to select it; then click on the upper right-arrow pointing to the "Dependent Variable" box; **time** disappears from the left-hand box and reappears under "Dependent Variable." Next, click on **attract** (our first independent variable) to select it, and then click on the right-arrow button pointing to the "Fixed Factor(s)" box to move it there.

Now repeat these steps to select the second independent variable (factor), **approach**. Click on **approach** in the left-hand box, and then on the arrow pointing to the "Fixed Factor(s)" box to move it there.

If you wish to have SPSS print out means and standard deviations for your six cells in addition to the results of the *F*-test—and of course you do!—click on the button labeled **Options**, which produces a new dialog box as illustrated in Figure 11.2. The only option we're interested in here appears in the lower-left corner of the dialog box: Click on the box to the left of the

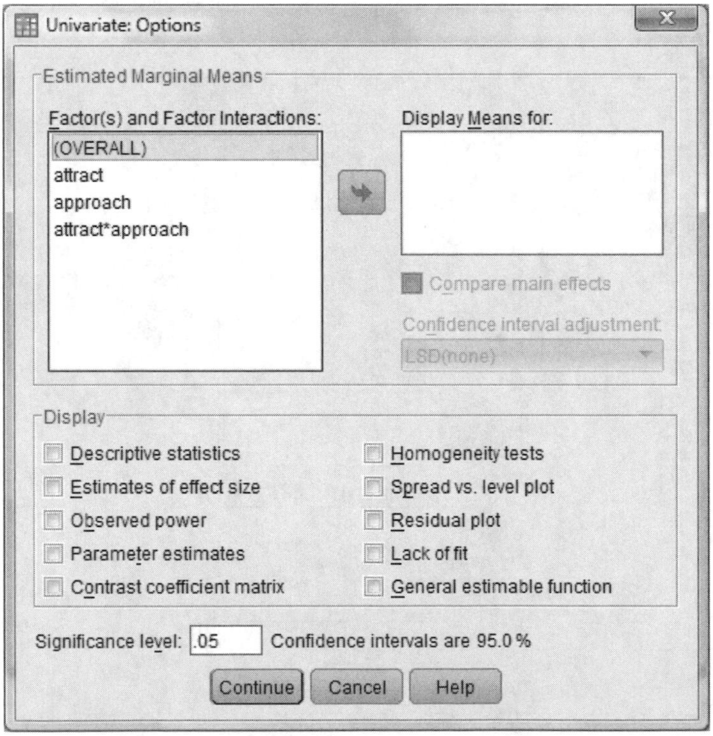

**Figure 11.2**

phrase "Descriptive statistics." This tells SPSS to print out your cell means and standard deviations. Click on **Continue** to return to the dialog box illustrated in Figure 11.1, and then click on **OK** to run the analysis.

As part of the "Descriptive Statistics" output, SPSS will print out the *weighted* marginal means for your independent variables. If you wish to see *unweighted* marginal means, however, you need to request them explicitly. (Recall that if *n*'s are all equal, these two kinds of marginal means will be identical and requesting the unweighted means is not necessary.) To do so, follow the instructions in the preceding paragraph to request "Descriptive statistics," but before clicking on **Continue**, you need to do one more thing in this dialog box. Click on the word **attract** in the upper-left corner of the dialog box (see Figure 11.2) to highlight the word, and then click on the arrow in the upper-center of the box so that **attract** appears in the right-hand list. Then move **approach** in the same way. Now click on **Continue**, and then on **OK** to run the analysis.

Syntax Method

Open the Syntax Editor, type the following command (don't forget the period at the end!), and then click on the *Run* button to execute the analysis:

```
GLM TIME BY ATTRACT APPROACH /PRINT = DESCRIPTIVE.
```

The **GLM** command in SPSS can be used to analyze univariate as well as multivariate designs (those with several dependent variables). Here, we are using the **GLM** command to conduct a two-way analysis of variance.

After the **GLM** command, you must type the name of your dependent variable. In this example, the dependent variable is **TIME**. Then type the word **BY**, followed by the names of your between-subjects factors (that is, the independent variables). In this example, the independent variables are **ATTRACT** and **APPROACH**.

The **/PRINT = DESCRIPTIVE** subcommand tells SPSS to produce the observed means and other descriptive statistics on the dependent variable for each of the cells in the design.

As part of the output from **/PRINT = DESCRIPTIVE**, SPSS will print out the *weighted* marginal means for your independent variables. If you wish to see *unweighted* marginal means, however, you need to request them explicitly. (Recall that if *n*'s are all equal, these two kinds of marginal means will be identical and requesting the unweighted means is not necessary.) To do so, add the following two subcommands to your **GLM** (or **UNIANOVA**) command, in addition to the **/PRINT = DESCRIPTIVE** subcommand:

```
/EMMEANS = TABLES (ATTRACT)
/EMMEANS = TABLES (APPROACH)
```

# Output

If you requested descriptive statistics, part of your output will look like Figure 11.3. (The section of output labeled "Descriptive Statistics" will not appear if you did not request these statistics.)

The cell means, standard deviations, and sample sizes ("N") of the dependent variable *time* are produced for each combination of levels of the independent variables. The arrangement in which the means are printed is a bit awkward, however, and makes it difficult to "see" the main effects. These means might better be arranged, in accordance with the two-way nature of the design, as follows:

|  |  | APPROACH | | | |
|---|---|---|---|---|---|
|  |  | 1 = Conversation | 2 = Humor | 3 = Pick-Up Line | |
| A T T R A C T | 1 = Attractive | 41.60 | 48.00 | 2.40 | 30.67 |
|  | 2 = Unattractive | 18.80 | 46.80 | 2.20 | 22.60 |
|  |  | 30.20 | 47.40 | 2.30 | |

The cell means in the table above were taken directly from the "Descriptive Statistics" section of Figure 11.3. The marginal means can also be found there, in the various rows labeled "Total." For example, the means of the three groups for whom *attract* = 1 were 41.60, 48.00, and 2.40. Adding these three means together and dividing by 3 yields 30.67, the marginal mean for *attract* group 1. In Figure 11.3, this value appears in the first row labeled "Total" in the "Descriptive Statistics" section.

If (unlike our example) the $n$'s for the various cells were unequal, the marginal means presented in the "Descriptive Statistics" section of the output would correspond to *weighted* means. These may not be the most appropriate marginal means to examine in assessing your main effects when $n$'s are unequal. The *unweighted* marginal means, which are printed only if you followed the appropriate procedures described earlier, will appear separately at the end of the output. These results are discussed later in this section.

The last section of output contains results of the significance tests, under "Tests of Between-Subjects Effects." The line labeled "Error" refers to the "error term" used in all of the $F$-tests. In this example, $SS_{error} = 1154.800$, $df_{error} = 24$, and $MS_{error}$ (found by dividing $SS_{error}$ by $df_{error}$) = 48.117. This last value is used as the denominator in the $F$ ratios for testing the main effects and interaction.

The three sources of variability of primary interest are: (1) "attract," which refers to the main effect of attractiveness; (2) "approach," which refers to the main effect of approach type; and (3) "attract * approach," which refers to the interaction of the two independent variables. For each, the sums of

# General Linear Model

## Between-Subjects Factors

|          |   | N  |
|----------|---|----|
| attract  | 1 | 15 |
|          | 2 | 15 |
| approach | 1 | 10 |
|          | 2 | 10 |
|          | 3 | 10 |

## Descriptive Statistics

Dependent Variable: time

| attract | approach | Mean  | Std. Deviation | N  |
|---------|----------|-------|----------------|----|
| 1       | 1        | 41.60 | 9.072          | 5  |
|         | 2        | 48.00 | 8.660          | 5  |
|         | 3        | 2.40  | 1.140          | 5  |
|         | Total    | 30.67 | 21.924         | 15 |
| 2       | 1        | 18.80 | 6.535          | 5  |
|         | 2        | 46.80 | 9.257          | 5  |
|         | 3        | 2.20  | 1.304          | 5  |
|         | Total    | 22.60 | 20.003         | 15 |
| Total   | 1        | 30.20 | 14.141         | 10 |
|         | 2        | 47.40 | 8.475          | 10 |
|         | 3        | 2.30  | 1.160          | 10 |
|         | Total    | 26.63 | 21.025         | 30 |

## Tests of Between-Subjects Effects

Dependent Variable: time

| Source            | Type III Sum of Squares | df | Mean Square | F       | Sig. |
|-------------------|-------------------------|----|-------------|---------|------|
| Corrected Model   | 11664.167[a]            | 5  | 2332.833    | 48.483  | .000 |
| Intercept         | 21280.033               | 1  | 21280.033   | 442.259 | .000 |
| attract           | 488.033                 | 1  | 488.033     | 10.143  | .004 |
| approach          | 10360.867               | 2  | 5180.433    | 107.664 | .000 |
| attract * approach| 815.267                 | 2  | 407.633     | 8.472   | .002 |
| Error             | 1154.800                | 24 | 48.117      |         |      |
| Total             | 34099.000               | 30 |             |         |      |
| Corrected Total   | 12818.967               | 29 |             |         |      |

a. R Squared = .910 (Adjusted R Squared = .891)

Figure 11.3

squares ("Type III Sum of Squares"), degrees of freedom ("df"), and mean square are reported, along with the $F$ ratios and $p$-values ("Sig.") for the significance tests. Each $F$ is calculated as the ratio of the mean square for a particular effect divided by the $MS_{error}$ (48.117). In this problem, the three $F$ ratios are as follows:

$$F_{Attract} = \frac{488.033}{48.117} = 10.143; F_{Approach} = \frac{5180.433}{48.117} = 107.664; F_{Inter} = \frac{407.633}{48.117} = 8.472$$

The $p$-values for these $F$ ratios are listed under "Sig." and in this example equal .004, .000 (that is, less than .0005), and .002, respectively. Thus, in this case, all three $p$-values are sufficiently small to reject the respective null hypotheses at the .05 or .01 level. That is, for each main effect and interaction, $p < .05$ and also $p < .01$; all three effects are statistically significant.

Unweighted Marginal Means for Main Effects

If you followed one of the procedures for requesting unweighted marginal means, the last part of your output will look like Figure 11.4. SPSS refers to these as "estimated marginal means."

Note that in Figure 11.4, the marginal means for the two *attract* groups (30.667 and 22.600) and for the three *approach* groups (30.200, 47.400, and

# Estimated Marginal Means

### 1. attract

Dependent Variable: time

| attract | Mean | Std. Error | 95% Confidence Interval | |
|---|---|---|---|---|
| | | | Lower Bound | Upper Bound |
| 1 | 30.667 | 1.791 | 26.970 | 34.363 |
| 2 | 22.600 | 1.791 | 18.904 | 26.296 |

### 2. approach

Dependent Variable: time

| approach | Mean | Std. Error | 95% Confidence Interval | |
|---|---|---|---|---|
| | | | Lower Bound | Upper Bound |
| 1 | 30.200 | 2.194 | 25.673 | 34.727 |
| 2 | 47.400 | 2.194 | 42.873 | 51.927 |
| 3 | 2.300 | 2.194 | -2.227 | 6.827 |

**Figure 11.4**

2.300) agree with the marginal means discussed previously. Recall that this is only because, in our example, the cell $n$'s were all equal. If the $n$'s had been unequal, the (unweighted) marginal means in this table—which are the ones recommended by experts for most situations—would probably differ from the (weighted) marginal means in the "Descriptive Statistics" section of the output.

# Chapter 12

# One-Way Within-Subjects (Repeated Measures) ANOVA

## Sample Problem

The facilitator of a stress management therapy group conducted a study to determine the most effective relaxation technique(s) for stress reduction. The 20 members of his stress management group participated in the study. The heart rate of each participant was monitored during each of five conditions. Each participant experienced all five conditions during the same session to control for variations in the amount of stress experienced from day to day. The five conditions are as follows: (1) baseline (subjects sat quietly for 15 minutes); (2) guided meditation (subjects listened to a tape instructing them to close their eyes, breathe deeply, and relax their muscles for 15 minutes while concentrating on a single word or phrase); (3) comedy (subjects listened to the act of a stand-up comedian on a tape cassette for 15 minutes); (4) nature (subjects listened to a tape for 15 minutes of various sounds of nature, including the sounds of the ocean, wind, rain, leaves rustling, and birds chirping); and (5) music (subjects listened to a tape of a collection of easy-listening music for 15 minutes). Every subject experienced the baseline condition first; however, the four treatment conditions were counterbalanced to alleviate the possibility of any order effects. Each subject's heart rate was monitored continuously during each of the 15-minute periods. The mean heart rate (beats per minute) for each subject during each condition is as follows:

| Subject | Baseline | Meditation | Comedy | Nature | Music |
|---------|----------|------------|--------|--------|-------|
| 1       | 85       | 70         | 75     | 71     | 74    |
| 2       | 79       | 69         | 73     | 70     | 72    |
| 3       | 91       | 82         | 87     | 83     | 86    |
| 4       | 93       | 80         | 85     | 79     | 84    |
| 5       | 92       | 80         | 86     | 81     | 87    |
| 6       | 87       | 79         | 83     | 80     | 81    |
| 7       | 84       | 72         | 77     | 73     | 76    |
| 8       | 78       | 69         | 74     | 71     | 73    |
| 9       | 79       | 69         | 73     | 70     | 72    |
| 10      | 80       | 71         | 74     | 72     | 73    |
| 11      | 80       | 72         | 76     | 74     | 75    |
| 12      | 97       | 80         | 89     | 82     | 87    |
| 13      | 88       | 78         | 82     | 80     | 82    |
| 14      | 94       | 79         | 84     | 80     | 84    |
| 15      | 75       | 60         | 68     | 62     | 66    |
| 16      | 76       | 67         | 72     | 69     | 70    |
| 17      | 90       | 77         | 83     | 76     | 83    |

| Subject | Baseline | Meditation | Comedy | Nature | Music |
|---|---|---|---|---|---|
| 18 | 86 | 75 | 80 | 77 | 80 |
| 19 | 94 | 84 | 88 | 85 | 87 |
| 20 | 70 | 59 | 64 | 58 | 62 |

In this problem, we are testing the null hypothesis that, on average, the heart rates of subjects remain the same during each of the five conditions (the baseline condition and the four relaxation conditions). That is, the population means for all five conditions are equal or, alternatively, these conditions do not influence heart rate differently.

## Analysis

Following the procedure outlined in Chapter 2, enter the data into the first six columns of the Data Editor and label the variables **subject**, **baseline**, **meditate**, **comedy**, **nature**, and **music**.

Point-and-Click Method

Click on **Analyze** on the menu bar, then choose **General Linear Model** from the pull-down menu, and then choose **Repeated Measures**. This produces a dialog box that looks like Figure 12.1.

**Figure 12.1**

Although you entered the data so that **baseline**, **meditate**, and so forth represent five different variables, the trick to running a within-subjects ANOVA is to make SPSS understand that these are not to be thought of as five different variables, but rather as scores from five different *levels* of a single within-subject independent variable that we will call **cond** (for "condition"). The scores (heart rates) themselves, which vary from condition to condition, represent the dependent variable. To accomplish this, click on the box next to "Within-Subject Factor Name," where the word **factor1** appears. SPSS calls the independent variable "factor1" unless we change this, so edit this box to say **cond** instead. Then click on the box beneath this, which is labeled "Number of Levels," and type the number **5**. This tells SPSS that the independent variable (now called **cond**) has five levels. Finally, click on the **Add** button (which becomes available or active after the previous two steps). You'll see **cond(5)** appear in the large box, confirming that you did the previous two steps correctly.

Now we must tell SPSS what those five levels of **cond** are—that is, which variables in your data represent those five levels. To do so, click on **Define** to produce the dialog box illustrated in Figure 12.2.

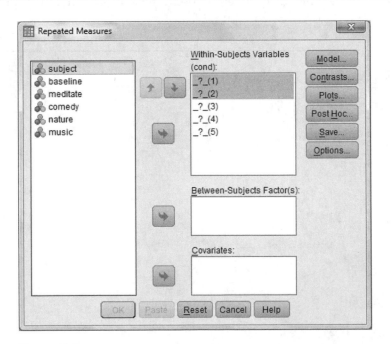

**Figure 12.2**

The names of all your variables appear in the box to the left, and the large box in the center labeled "Within-Subjects Variables [cond]" looks like some kind of form waiting to be filled out—which it is. There are five slots containing question marks, and you fill them in by selecting the variables that represent scores from the five levels of your independent variable. To do this, click on the name of the first condition, **baseline**, and then click on the right-arrow button pointing to the "Within-Subjects Variables [cond]" box. The slot containing the question mark now says **baseline[1]**, confirming that the variable **baseline** corresponds to the first level of the within-subjects independent variable. Now repeat this procedure, in order, to move **meditate**, **comedy**, **nature**, and **music** in the same way. When finished, all five of these variables should appear in the "Within-Subjects Variables [cond]" box.

Before clicking on **OK**, there is one more step: Click on the **Options . . .** button (at the right of the dialog box) to produce a new dialog box (not pictured), and then click on the little square next to the word "Descriptives." This tells SPSS to print out your cell means and standard deviations. Ignoring the rest of this box, click on **Continue** to return to the main dialog box, and click on **OK** to run the analysis.

### Syntax Method

Open the Syntax Editor, type the following command (don't forget the period at the end!), and then click on the *Run* button to execute the analysis. (Note that we have used multiple lines and indentation for clarity, but this is optional.)

```
GLM BASELINE MEDITATE COMEDY NATURE MUSIC
  /WSFACTORS = COND (5)
  /PRINT = DESCRIPTIVE.
```

The **GLM** command in SPSS can be used to analyze a variety of univariate and multivariate designs, including those in which the same variable is measured more than once for each subject. Here, we are using the **GLM** command to conduct a one-way within-subjects (repeated measures) analysis of variance.

When conducting a repeated measures analysis using **GLM**, you must set up your data so that the repeated measurements exist as different variables. Notice that, although we are measuring the same thing (heart rate) for each subject under all five conditions, the data values are entered as if there were five separate variables. Each of these variables represents a different level of the within-subjects factor (heart rate).

After the **GLM** command, you must type the names of the dependent variables that represent the various conditions or levels of the independent variable. In this example, our variable names are **BASELINE**, **MEDITATE**, **COMEDY**, **NATURE**, and **MUSIC**. Each dependent variable listed represents heart rate measured at different times for the same subject.

The subcommand **/WSFACTORS** (within-subjects factors) must be the first subcommand typed after the variable names. Then you must type a name for your within-subjects factor. This *cannot* be the name of one of your existing variables. In this example, we chose the name **COND** (for "condition") for the independent variable. Next, you must type, in parentheses, the number of levels for the within-subjects factor. In this example, heart rate is being measured under five different conditions; therefore, there are **(5)** levels of our within-subjects factor **COND**. (This tells SPSS that we do not really have five separate dependent variables, but rather scores from five levels of one independent variable called **COND**.)

The **/PRINT = DESCRIPTIVE** (observed means) subcommand tells SPSS to produce the observed means for each level of the within-subjects factor (that is, for each variable listed on the command).

## Output

The output produced by SPSS for this analysis is reproduced in Figure 12.3.

The first section of output (not shown), labeled "Within-Subjects Factors," simply lists the five variables representing the five treatment conditions to confirm that you specified the analysis correctly. This is followed immediately by "Descriptive Statistics," which lists the mean, standard deviation, and N for each of these. In this case, the means for the 20 participants range from a low of 73.60 (*meditate* condition) to a high of 84.90 (*baseline* condition).

The next section, labeled "Multivariate Tests," may be of interest only to advanced users. The tests in this section—labeled "Pillai's Trace," "Wilks' Lambda," and so on—are all tests of the *cond* effect conducted using *multivariate* (MANOVA) techniques. This method for conducting repeated measures analysis of variance is entirely different from the more familiar *univariate*, sums-of-squares method taught in most textbooks. In this particular case, all of these multivariate tests happen to agree perfectly with one another, but this will not always be true. Each of these tests would lead one to conclude that there is a significant *cond* effect (that is, "Sig." is listed as .000, which is less than the traditional alpha level of .05 or .01).

The next section of the printout, labeled "Mauchly's Test of Sphericity," contains a variety of statistics that also are probably of interest only to advanced users. This chi-square test is intended to test the hypothesis that the "sphericity assumption" underlying the univariate $F$-tests is met. (In this example, the test is significant—"Sig." is reported as .000—indicating that the assumption appears to be violated.) To the right of this are three values of a statistic called "epsilon," which are used to make corrections to the univariate $F$-tests when the sphericity assumption appears to be violated. Because SPSS will calculate these corrections and report the results of the adjusted tests in a subsequent section, you probably will not have any need to know the actual values of these epsilon statistics.

# General Linear Model

**Descriptive Statistics**

| | Mean | Std. Deviation | N |
|---|---|---|---|
| baseline | 84.90 | 7.511 | 20 |
| meditate | 73.60 | 6.969 | 20 |
| comedy | 78.65 | 7.036 | 20 |
| nature | 74.65 | 7.006 | 20 |
| music | 77.70 | 7.420 | 20 |

**Multivariate Tests[b]**

| Effect | | Value | F | Hypothesis df | Error df | Sig. |
|---|---|---|---|---|---|---|
| cond | Pillai's Trace | .960 | 96.561[a] | 4.000 | 16.000 | .000 |
| | Wilks' Lambda | .040 | 96.561[a] | 4.000 | 16.000 | .000 |
| | Hotelling's Trace | 24.140 | 96.561[a] | 4.000 | 16.000 | .000 |
| | Roy's Largest Root | 24.140 | 96.561[a] | 4.000 | 16.000 | .000 |

a. Exact statistic

b. Design: Intercept
Within Subjects Design: cond

**Figure 12.3**

(continued on next page)

**Mauchly's Test of Sphericity[b]**

Measure: MEASURE_1

| Within Subjects Effect | Mauchly's W | Approx. Chi-Square | df | Sig. | Epsilon[a] | | |
|---|---|---|---|---|---|---|---|
| | | | | | Greenhouse-Geisser | Huynh-Feldt | Lower-bound |
| cond | .077 | 44.681 | 9 | .000 | .414 | .448 | .250 |

Tests the null hypothesis that the error covariance matrix of the orthonormalized transformed dependent variables is proportional to an identity matrix.

a. May be used to adjust the degrees of freedom for the averaged tests of significance. Corrected tests are displayed in the Tests of Within–Subjects Effects table.

b.
  Design: Intercept
  Within Subjects Design: cond

**Tests of Within-Subjects Effects**

Measure: MEASURE_1

| Source | | Type III Sum of Squares | df | Mean Square | F | Sig. |
|---|---|---|---|---|---|---|
| cond | Sphericity Assumed | 1573.100 | 4 | 393.275 | 235.531 | .000 |
| | Greenhouse-Geisser | 1573.100 | 1.654 | 951.015 | 235.531 | .000 |
| | Huynh-Feldt | 1573.100 | 1.792 | 877.881 | 235.531 | .000 |
| | Lower-bound | 1573.100 | 1.000 | 1573.100 | 235.531 | .000 |
| Error(cond) | Sphericity Assumed | 126.900 | 76 | 1.670 | | |
| | Greenhouse-Geisser | 126.900 | 31.428 | 4.038 | | |
| | Huynh-Feldt | 126.900 | 34.047 | 3.727 | | |
| | Lower-bound | 126.900 | 19.000 | 6.679 | | |

**Figure 12.3** (*continued*)

(continued on next page)

**Tests of Within-Subjects Contrasts**

Measure: MEASURE_1

| Source | cond | Type III Sum of Squares | df | Mean Square | F | Sig. |
|---|---|---|---|---|---|---|
| cond | Linear | 356.445 | 1 | 356.445 | 222.376 | .000 |
| | Quadratic | 551.604 | 1 | 551.604 | 231.229 | .000 |
| | Cubic | 172.980 | 1 | 172.980 | 309.475 | .000 |
| | Order 4 | 492.071 | 1 | 492.071 | 230.848 | .000 |
| Error(cond) | Linear | 30.455 | 19 | 1.603 | | |
| | Quadratic | 45.325 | 19 | 2.386 | | |
| | Cubic | 10.620 | 19 | .559 | | |
| | Order 4 | 40.500 | 19 | 2.132 | | |

**Tests of Between-Subjects Effects**

Measure: MEASURE_1
Transformed Variable: Average

| Source | Type III Sum of Squares | df | Mean Square | F | Sig. |
|---|---|---|---|---|---|
| Intercept | 606841.000 | 1 | 606841.000 | 2408.602 | .000 |
| Error | 4787.000 | 19 | 251.947 | | |

**Figure 12.3** (*continued*)

The next section of the results—labeled "Tests of Within-Subjects Effects"—presents the more familiar univariate test of the hypothesis of interest. The upper half of this table, labeled "cond," contains several versions of the $F$-test for the *cond* effect. The first line is the standard, univariate test that most students learn to compute by hand; it is labeled "Sphericity Assumed" because if this assumption about the population is violated, the $F$-test will be inaccurate. The next three lines report different kinds of corrected $F$-tests ("Greenhouse-Geisser," and so on) that have been developed for cases in which the sphericity assumption appears to be violated. (These involve making adjustments to the degrees of freedom; note that the df values differ from row to row.)

In each case, the error term for the respective $F$-test is given in the lower half of the table, in the section labeled "Error(cond)." In this example, the $F$ ratio for the uncorrected ("Sphericity Assumed") test equals 235.531, the result of dividing $MS_{cond}$ (393.275, from upper half of table) by $MS_{error}$ (1.670, from lower half of table); the associated $p$-value is less than .0005. (Remember, a $p$-value printed as ".000" has just been rounded off.) The null hypothesis is rejected; condition does appear to have an effect on measured heart rates. In this example, the same conclusion would be reached based on any of the corrected tests as well.

The remaining sections of the printout are probably not of interest to most users. The section labeled "Tests of Within-Subjects Contrasts" breaks down the *cond* effect into a set of orthogonal contrasts and provides a significance test for each. By default, these contrasts are constructed according to a so-called trend analysis. In the present example, this particular set of contrasts is probably meaningless, but in many cases (such as when the repeated measures factor represents differences across time), they may be useful. There are ways to ask SPSS to construct these contrasts in other ways instead, but this topic is beyond the scope of the present manual. The last section, labeled "Tests of Between-Subjects Effects," is not of interest in this example because in this one-way design there were no between-subjects independent variables. The only $F$-test printed here is for something called "Intercept," which generally is of no interest. (In case you are curious, this is a test of the hypothesis that the overall mean heart rate in the population equals zero. This is clearly a meaningless hypothesis in the present case and it should come as no surprise that it is "significant.")

Within-subjects ANOVA is a very complex topic, as evidenced by the fact that the printout produced no fewer than eight different tests of the same null hypothesis. Depending on various factors, some of these may agree with each other and some will not. Which one should you use? Because the topic is so complex, it is beyond the scope of this manual. Nevertheless, we offer a few brief comments. First, because violations of the sphericity assumption can severely bias the uncorrected, univariate test ("Sphericity Assumed"), in most cases it is probably best not to rely on this result. Among the univariate tests, most textbooks instead recommend using a corrected test based on either the "Greenhouse-Geisser" or "Huynh-Feldt" adjustment. Second, it should be noted that multivariate tests are becoming increasingly popular as an alternative to the more traditional univariate tests; they are generally safer because they do not rely on the sphericity assumption at all. Among these tests, the most commonly used versions are probably those based on "Pillai's Trace" and "Wilks' Lambda."

# Chapter 13

# Two-Way Mixed (Between-Within) ANOVA

## Sample Problem

An adult attachment researcher read an article describing the effects of inse-cure attachment on the physiology of sleep in children. This researcher found the results to be very compelling and hypothesized that similar effects may be observed in romantic couples. Therefore, he conducted a similar study to empirically demonstrate the effects of secure romantic attachment on the physiology of sleep. Previous research had indicated that periods of almost any kind of anxiety or stress are associated with sleep disturbances, such as a reduction in deep (delta) sleep; individuals who are stressed exhibit a tendency toward less and lighter sleep. For this study, the researcher wanted to determine whether the presence of a romantic partner while sleeping reduces the presence of sleep disturbances in individuals who are stressed. Thirty women who had recently moved to a new area to begin new jobs and their romantic partners were selected for participation in the study. The sleep patterns of 10 secure, 10 anxious, and 10 avoidant women were monitored while they slept alone and while they slept with their romantic partners. Of primary importance to the attachment researcher was the overall percentage of time that each subject spent in deep delta sleep. The investigator hypoth-esized that all subjects will experience sleep disturbances in the absence of their romantic partners due to the stressful nature of their present circum-stances. However, it was hypothesized that subjects with secure attachment styles will derive comfort from the presence of their romantic partners and will sleep better (experience more delta sleep) than subjects with insecure attachment styles. Following is the average amount of time that each subject spent in delta sleep in each partner-proximity condition, expressed as a per-centage of total sleep time. (For attachment styles, 1 = secure, 2 = anxious, and 3 = avoidant.)

| Subject | Attachment Style | Partner-Absent Delta | Partner-Present Delta |
|---|---|---|---|
| 1 | 1 | 17 | 22 |
| 2 | 1 | 16 | 25 |
| 3 | 1 | 15 | 21 |
| 4 | 1 | 18 | 23 |
| 5 | 1 | 19 | 22 |
| 6 | 1 | 20 | 25 |
| 7 | 1 | 17 | 22 |
| 8 | 1 | 15 | 21 |
| 9 | 1 | 16 | 23 |

| Subject | Attachment Style | Partner-Absent Delta | Partner-Present Delta |
|---------|------------------|----------------------|-----------------------|
| 10 | 1 | 15 | 22 |
| 11 | 2 | 14 | 15 |
| 12 | 2 | 15 | 17 |
| 13 | 2 | 17 | 17 |
| 14 | 2 | 19 | 20 |
| 15 | 2 | 15 | 18 |
| 16 | 2 | 14 | 15 |
| 17 | 2 | 15 | 14 |
| 18 | 2 | 13 | 15 |
| 19 | 2 | 15 | 14 |
| 20 | 2 | 15 | 16 |
| 21 | 3 | 19 | 20 |
| 22 | 3 | 15 | 15 |
| 23 | 3 | 15 | 15 |
| 24 | 3 | 17 | 18 |
| 25 | 3 | 18 | 18 |
| 26 | 3 | 19 | 19 |
| 27 | 3 | 15 | 16 |
| 28 | 3 | 15 | 17 |
| 29 | 3 | 17 | 15 |
| 30 | 3 | 16 | 16 |

In this example, we are conducting a two-way mixed analysis of variance with one within-subjects factor and one between-groups factor. Partner-proximity is a within-subjects factor because each subject's sleep patterns were monitored both in the presence and in the absence of their romantic partners. Attachment style is a between-groups factor because it subdivides the sample into three discrete subgroups; each subject has only one attachment style (secure, anxious, or avoidant).

As in any two-way analysis of variance, three different null hypotheses (two main effects and an interaction) are tested. The three null hypotheses that we are testing in this problem are as follows:

1. There is no main effect of attachment style. There is no difference in the mean percentage of delta sleep for the three populations of secure, anxious, and avoidant women.
2. There is no main effect of partner-proximity. There is no difference in mean percentage of delta sleep for subjects in the two partner-proximity conditions; subjects spend an equal percentage of time in delta sleep when their romantic partners are present and when they are absent.
3. There is no interaction (attachment style × partner-proximity). The effect of attachment style is independent of partner-proximity. The effects of the factor attachment style are consistent across all levels of partner-proximity.

## Analysis

Following the procedure outlined in Chapter 2, enter the data into the first four columns of the Data Editor and label the variables **subject**, **attstyle**, **padelta**, and **ppdelta**.

### Point-and-Click Method

The first part of the procedure involves specifying the within-subjects (repeated measures) independent variable and is the same as the procedure for the simple within-subjects design. That is, click on **Analyze** on the menu bar, then choose **General Linear Model** from the pull-down menu, and then choose **Repeated Measures.**

Begin by temporarily pretending that you are running a simple within-subjects design, with **partner** (present versus absent) as your independent variable, and ignoring (for the moment) the variable **attachment style**. Follow the instructions in Chapter 12 to specify your "Within-Subject Factor Name" to be **partner** (rather than **cond**, as in Chapter 12), and specify the "Number of Levels" as **2** (rather than **5**, as in Chapter 12). Then **Define** the within-subject factor by choosing **padelta** and **ppdelta** (rather than **baseline**, **meditate**, and so on, as in Chapter 12).

Because this is a mixed design, we still need to specify a between-subjects independent variable. Below the "Within-Subjects Variables [cond]" box is a smaller one labeled "Between-Subjects Factor(s)." As you probably guessed, you specify this variable by clicking on the appropriate variable from the list on the left, in this case **attstyle**, and then clicking on the arrow key pointing to the "Between-Subjects Factor(s)" box.

Finally, you can obtain your cell means and standard deviations as explained in Chapter 12. That is, click on **Options . . .** and choose "Descriptives" from the resulting dialog box. Then click on **Continue** to return to the main dialog box and then click on **OK** to run the analysis.

### Syntax Method

Open the Syntax Editor, type the following command (don't forget the period at the end!), and then click on the *Run* button to execute the analysis. (Note that we have used multiple lines and indentation for clarity, but this is optional.)

```
GLM PADELTA PPDELTA BY ATTSTYLE
 /WSFACTORS = PARTNER (2)
 /PRINT = DESCRIPTIVE.
```

The **GLM** command was used previously for both between-subjects factorial designs (Chapter 11) and one-way within-subjects designs (Chapter 12). For this mixed factorial design, notice that the command syntax combines elements from both of these previous applications. The **BY ATTSTYLE** part of the command specifies the between-subjects variable; the **/WSFACTORS** subcommand specifies the within-subjects (repeated measures) variable; the **/PRINT = DESCRIPTIVE** subcommand requests descriptive statistics. See Chapters 11 and 12 for more detailed discussion.

## Output

Portions of the output produced by SPSS for this analysis are reproduced in Figure 13.1.

The first two sections of output (not shown), labeled "Within-Subjects Factors" and "Between-Subjects Factors," simply list the variables representing your independent variables to confirm that you specified the analysis correctly. In the first table, *padelta* and *ppdelta* are listed as the variables representing the two levels of the within-subjects variable, and *attstyle* is listed as the between-subjects variable. These tables are followed immediately by "Descriptive Statistics," which lists the mean, standard deviation, and *N* for each of the three groups on each of the two measures (see Figure 13.1). In this case, for example, the means on *padelta* are 16.80, 15.20, and 16.60, respectively, for the three *attstyle* groups.

The next table, labeled "Multivariate Tests," may be of interest only to advanced users. The table is divided into two sections. The tests in the upper half are tests of the *partner* main effect; those in the bottom half are tests of the *partner * attstyle* interaction. In general, this table will include a section for every main effect and interaction in your design that involves a within-subjects variable. Within each section are four different tests, discussed previously in Chapter 12, labeled "Pillai's Trace," "Wilks' Lambda," and so on; these are alternative tests of the given main effect or interaction using *multivari-*

## General Linear Model

**Descriptive Statistics**

|  | attstyle | Mean | Std. Deviation | N |
|---|---|---|---|---|
| padelta | 1 | 16.80 | 1.751 | 10 |
|  | 2 | 15.20 | 1.687 | 10 |
|  | 3 | 16.60 | 1.647 | 10 |
|  | Total | 16.20 | 1.789 | 30 |
| ppdelta | 1 | 22.60 | 1.430 | 10 |
|  | 2 | 16.10 | 1.912 | 10 |
|  | 3 | 16.90 | 1.792 | 10 |
|  | Total | 18.53 | 3.381 | 30 |

**Figure 13.1**

*(continued on next page)*

**Multivariate Tests[b]**

| Effect | | Value | F | Hypothesis df | Error df | Sig. |
|---|---|---|---|---|---|---|
| partner | Pillai's Trace | .771 | 90.741[a] | 1.000 | 27.000 | .000 |
| | Wilks' Lambda | .229 | 90.741[a] | 1.000 | 27.000 | .000 |
| | Hotelling's Trace | 3.361 | 90.741[a] | 1.000 | 27.000 | .000 |
| | Roy's Largest Root | 3.361 | 90.741[a] | 1.000 | 27.000 | .000 |
| partner * attstyle | Pillai's Trace | .789 | 50.574[a] | 2.000 | 27.000 | .000 |
| | Wilks' Lambda | .211 | 50.574[a] | 2.000 | 27.000 | .000 |
| | Hotelling's Trace | 3.746 | 50.574[a] | 2.000 | 27.000 | .000 |
| | Roy's Largest Root | 3.746 | 50.574[a] | 2.000 | 27.000 | .000 |

a. Exact statistic

b.
  Design: Intercept+attstyle
  Within Subjects Design: partner

**Tests of Within-Subjects Effects**

Measure: MEASURE_1

| Source | | Type III Sum of Squares | df | Mean Square | F | Sig. |
|---|---|---|---|---|---|---|
| partner | Sphericity Assumed | 81.667 | 1 | 81.667 | 90.741 | .000 |
| | Greenhouse-Geisser | 81.667 | 1.000 | 81.667 | 90.741 | .000 |
| | Huynh-Feldt | 81.667 | 1.000 | 81.667 | 90.741 | .000 |
| | Lower-bound | 81.667 | 1.000 | 81.667 | 90.741 | .000 |
| partner * attstyle | Sphericity Assumed | 91.033 | 2 | 45.517 | 50.574 | .000 |
| | Greenhouse-Geisser | 91.033 | 2.000 | 45.517 | 50.574 | .000 |
| | Huynh-Feldt | 91.033 | 2.000 | 45.517 | 50.574 | .000 |
| | Lower-bound | 91.033 | 2.000 | 45.517 | 50.574 | .000 |
| Error(partner) | Sphericity Assumed | 24.300 | 27 | .900 | | |
| | Greenhouse-Geisser | 24.300 | 27.000 | .900 | | |
| | Huynh-Feldt | 24.300 | 27.000 | .900 | | |
| | Lower-bound | 24.300 | 27.000 | .900 | | |

**Tests of Between-Subjects Effects**

Measure: MEASURE_1
Transformed Variable: Average

| Source | Type III Sum of Squares | df | Mean Square | F | Sig. |
|---|---|---|---|---|---|
| Intercept | 18096.067 | 1 | 18096.067 | 3659.879 | .000 |
| attstyle | 175.433 | 2 | 87.717 | 17.740 | .000 |
| Error | 133.500 | 27 | 4.944 | | |

**Figure 13.1** *(continued)*

*ate* (MANOVA) techniques. This method for conducting repeated measures analysis of variance is entirely different from the more familiar *univariate*, sums-of-squares method taught in most textbooks. In this particular case, all of these multivariate tests happen to agree perfectly with one another, but this will not always be true. For these data, both the *partner* effect and the *partner * attstyle* interaction are clearly significant ("Sig." is reported as .000) using a traditional alpha level of .05 or .01.

The next section of the printout (not shown), labeled "Mauchly's Test of Sphericity," contains a variety of statistics that also are probably of interest only to advanced users. For more information, see the discussion of this part of the printout in Chapter 12.

The next section of the results—labeled "Tests of Within-Subjects Effects"—presents the more familiar univariate tests of the main effects and interactions that involve within-subjects variables. The upper part of this table, labeled "partner," contains several versions of the *F*-test for the *partner* main effect; the middle part contains corresponding tests for the *partner * attstyle* interaction. Within each of these sections, the first line is the standard, univariate test that most students learn to compute by hand; it is labeled "Sphericity Assumed" because if this assumption about the population is violated, the *F*-test will be inaccurate. The next three lines report different kinds of corrected *F*-tests ("Greenhouse-Geisser" and so on) that have been developed for cases in which the sphericity assumption appears to be violated.

In each case, the error term for the respective *F*-test is given in the bottom part of the table, in the section labeled "Error(partner)." In this mixed design, this represents the interaction of *partner * subjects* within groups and is used as the error term for tests of both the *partner* and *partner * attstyle* effects. For example, the *F* ratio for the uncorrected ("Sphericity Assumed") test of *partner* equals 90.741, the result of dividing $MS_{cond}$ (81.667, from the upper section of the table) by $MS_{error}$ (.900, from the bottom section of the table); the associated *p*-value is less than .0005. (Remember, a *p*-value printed as ".000" has just been rounded off.) The null hypothesis is rejected; condition does appear to have an effect on measured heart rates. In this example, the same conclusion would be reached based on any of the corrected tests as well. In addition, the *partner * attstyle* interaction is also significant according to all four tests.

It is important to note that in this particular example, the three corrected tests ("Greenhouse-Geisser" and so on) all produced exactly the same results as the uncorrected test. In addition, all of these results are also identical to the tests reported under "Multivariate Tests," which was just discussed. All of these results are equivalent in this case because in our sample problem, the within-subjects variable *partner* had only two levels (*padelta* and *ppdelta*). When the within-subjects variable has only two levels, two things are true that otherwise are not generally true: First, the multivariate tests are not really "multivariate" in a technical sense—mathematically, they are identical to univariate tests. Second, there is no possibility of the sphericity assumption being violated; therefore, there is nothing for the Greenhouse-Geisser and Huynh-Feldt corrections to "correct" for. However, if the within-subjects variable had had three or more levels, the univariate tests would probably differ from the multivariate tests, and the various univariate tests would probably differ from each other—as was the case in the simpler one-way within-subjects design discussed in Chapter 12. See the end of Chapter 12 for some general recommendations for interpreting results when the results of these various tests are not identical.

The next section of the printout is probably not of interest to most users, and thus is not shown here. This section is labeled "Tests of Within-Subjects Contrasts," and, in general, it breaks down each of the within-subjects effects into a set of orthogonal contrasts and provides a significance test for each. (See Chapter 12 for a discussion.) In the present example, the within-subjects factors cannot be subdivided into contrasts because *partner* had only two levels; as a result, the output printed by SPSS (not shown here) is redundant with the results previously discussed.

The last section of output contains "Tests of Between-Subjects Effects." In this example, there is only one such effect, that for *attstyle*. (There is also a test for something called "Intercept," but this is generally of no interest and can safely be ignored.) The row labeled "Error" refers to the error term used to test the between-subjects effect(s) and represents the variation of subjects within groups. For each source, the sum of squares ("Type III Sum of Squares"), degrees of freedom ("df"), and mean square are listed. In this case, the *F*-value for *attstyle* equals 17.740, with a *p*-value ("Sig.") reported as ".000"—that is, less than .0005. The main effect for *attstyle* in this case is significant. Note that, unlike the situation with the within-subjects variables, there is only one significance test for the between-subjects effect(s): There are no multivariate tests, nor are there any corrected (for example, Greenhouse-Geisser) univariate tests.

# Chapter 14

# Correlations

## Sample Problem

An aerobics instructor believes that, aside from the physical benefits of exercising (muscle tone, low body fat, weight control), there are also numerous mental/psychological advantages to engaging in a regular aerobic exercise program. She believes that regular aerobic exercise is related to greater mental acuity, stress reduction, high self-esteem, and greater overall life satisfaction. In order to test this hypothesis, she recruits a random sample of 30 adults to participate in her study. Each subject is asked to fill out a series of questionnaires consisting of the following: (1) a preliminary questionnaire asking subjects to report the average number of hours per week that they engage in some sort of aerobic exercise; (2) a self-esteem scale (higher scores indicate greater self-esteem); (3) a life satisfaction questionnaire to determine each subject's overall outlook on life (higher scores indicate greater life satisfaction); (4) a perceived stress questionnaire (subjects are asked to read a series of vignettes describing potentially stressful events and are asked to rate the degree to which they perceive each event as stressful—higher scores indicate greater stress); and (5) an intelligence test to determine the IQ of each subject. The results are as follows:

| Subject | Exercise | Self-Esteem | Satisfaction | Stress | IQ |
|---|---|---|---|---|---|
| 1 | 10 | 25 | 45 | 20 | 105 |
| 2 | 33 | 37 | 40 | 10 | 120 |
| 3 | 9 | 12 | 30 | 13 | 110 |
| 4 | 14 | 32 | 39 | 15 | 100 |
| 5 | 3 | 22 | 27 | 29 | 105 |
| 6 | 12 | 31 | 44 | 22 | 120 |
| 7 | 7 | 30 | 39 | 13 | 110 |
| 8 | 15 | 30 | 40 | 20 | 110 |
| 9 | 3 | 15 | 46 | 25 | 95 |
| 10 | 21 | 34 | 50 | 10 | 125 |
| 11 | 2 | 18 | 29 | 33 | 105 |
| 12 | 20 | 37 | 47 | 5 | 105 |
| 13 | 4 | 19 | 31 | 23 | 100 |
| 14 | 8 | 33 | 38 | 21 | 105 |
| 15 | 0 | 10 | 25 | 30 | 100 |
| 16 | 17 | 35 | 42 | 13 | 105 |
| 17 | 25 | 39 | 40 | 10 | 110 |
| 18 | 2 | 13 | 30 | 27 | 105 |
| 19 | 18 | 35 | 47 | 9 | 105 |
| 20 | 3 | 15 | 28 | 25 | 100 |

| Subject | Exercise | Self-Esteem | Satisfaction | Stress | IQ |
|---------|----------|-------------|--------------|--------|-----|
| 21 | 27 | 35 | 39 | 7 | 115 |
| 22 | 4 | 17 | 32 | 34 | 115 |
| 23 | 8 | 20 | 34 | 20 | 110 |
| 24 | 10 | 22 | 41 | 15 | 95 |
| 25 | 0 | 14 | 27 | 35 | 105 |
| 26 | 12 | 35 | 35 | 20 | 115 |
| 27 | 5 | 20 | 30 | 23 | 105 |
| 28 | 7 | 29 | 30 | 12 | 95 |
| 29 | 30 | 40 | 48 | 14 | 110 |
| 30 | 14 | 30 | 45 | 15 | 110 |

In this problem, we are interested in calculating the Pearson product-moment correlation between each pair of variables. In addition, for each pair, we wish to test the null hypothesis that the correlation between the variables in the population from which the sample was drawn equals zero.

## Analysis

Following the procedure outlined in Chapter 2, enter the data into the first six columns of the Data Editor and label the variables **subject**, **exercise**, **esteem**, **satisfy**, **stress**, and **iq**.

### Point-and-Click Method

Click on **Analyze** on the menu bar, and then choose **Correlate**. From the resulting menu, choose **Bivariate . . . .** This produces a dialog box that looks like Figure 14.1.

The rest is fairly self-explanatory. As in previous procedures, choose the variables you wish to include in the analyses by moving them from the box on the left to the box on the right (under "Variables"). In the present example, we wish to see the correlations among all of these variables except **subject**. Click on a variable name (say, **exercise**), and then click on the right-arrow key in the center of the dialog box. Then click on another variable name in the left-hand box, click on the right-arrow key, and repeat for as many variables as you wish to include. For the present example, we selected the variables in the order in which we entered them into the data window, but this is not necessary. The order of selection influences only the order in which the variables are listed in the output.

As you can see from Figure 14.1, clicking **OK** to run the analysis without changing anything else produces (1) Pearson correlation coefficients (rather than Kendall's tau-b or Spearman coefficients), (2) two-tailed rather than one-tailed significance tests, and (3) a display in which SPSS will "flag significant correlations." Click in the appropriate boxes to change any of these settings if

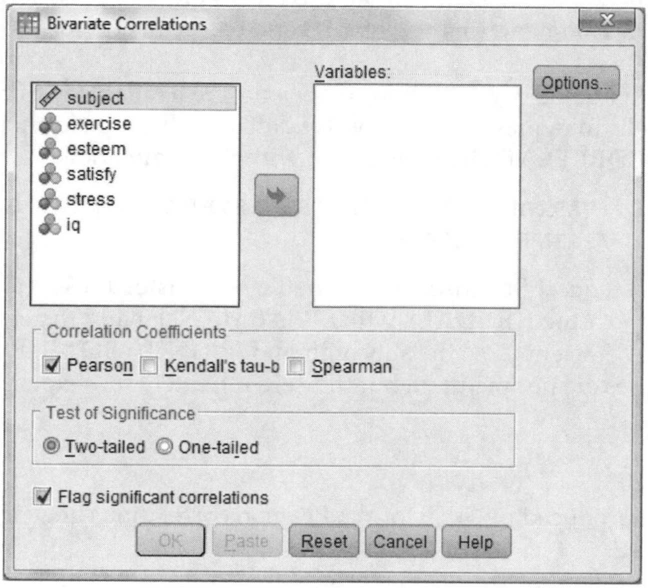

**Figure 14.1**

you wish; clicking on a box that is already selected (already has a check mark in it) will unselect it. ("Flag significant correlations" asks SPSS to print an asterisk next to each correlation that is significant at the .05 level, so you can locate these significant correlations easily when examining the output.)

If you wish to also see means and standard deviations for the variables selected, click on **Options . . .** , then click on the box labeled "Means and Standard Deviations" in the resulting dialog window (not shown). Click on **Continue** to exit this window, then on **OK** to run the analysis:

Syntax Method

Open the Syntax Editor, type the following command (don't forget the period at the end!), and then click on the *Run* button to execute the analysis:

```
CORRELATIONS /VARIABLES = EXERCISE ESTEEM SATISFY STRESS IQ.
```

The **CORRELATIONS** command is used to calculate the Pearson correlation coefficients between pairs of variables.

After the **CORRELATIONS** command, you must type the subcommand **/VARIABLES**, then type the names of the variables to be correlated. In this example, we want to correlate the variables **EXERCISE**, **ESTEEM**, **SATISFY**, **STRESS**, and **IQ**.

If you would also like to see means and standard deviations for the variables specified, add the subcommand /**STATISTICS = DESCRIPTIVES** to the end of the command (that is, after **IQ** and before the period—don't forget that period!).

Two other kinds of correlation coefficients are available in SPSS for Windows as well. To request a matrix of Kendall's tau-b coefficients, replace the preceding **CORRELATIONS** command with the command:

```
NONPAR CORR /VARIABLES = EXERCISE ESTEEM SATISFY STRESS IQ
            /PRINT = KENDALL.
```

Similarly, to request Spearman's rho coefficients instead, use the command just given, replacing **KENDALL** with **SPEARMAN**. Finally, to get matrices of both these coefficients, use the subcommand /**PRINT = BOTH**. Results from these analyses are not pictured, but they are relatively self-explanatory.

## Output

The output produced by SPSS for the Pearson correlations analysis is shown in Figure 14.2.

SPSS produces a correlation matrix showing the correlations between all possible pairs of variables and indicates the number of cases used to compute them.

## Correlations

**Correlations**

| | | exercise | esteem | satisfy | stress | iq |
|---|---|---|---|---|---|---|
| exercise | Pearson Correlation | 1 | .843 | .678 | -.788 | .524 |
| | Sig. (2-tailed) | . | .000 | .000 | .000 | .003 |
| | N | 30 | 30 | 30 | 30 | 30 |
| esteem | Pearson Correlation | .843 | 1 | .701 | -.747 | .423 |
| | Sig. (2-tailed) | .000 | . | .000 | .000 | .020 |
| | N | 30 | 30 | 30 | 30 | 30 |
| satisfy | Pearson Correlation | .678 | .701 | 1 | -.649 | .311 |
| | Sig. (2-tailed) | .000 | .000 | . | .000 | .095 |
| | N | 30 | 30 | 30 | 30 | 30 |
| stress | Pearson Correlation | -.788 | -.747 | -.649 | 1 | -.225 |
| | Sig. (2-tailed) | .000 | .000 | .000 | . | .231 |
| | N | 30 | 30 | 30 | 30 | 30 |
| iq | Pearson Correlation | .524 | .423 | .311 | -.225 | 1 |
| | Sig. (2-tailed) | .003 | .020 | .095 | .231 | . |
| | N | 30 | 30 | 30 | 30 | 30 |

**Figure 14.2**

In each cell of the correlation matrix—that is, at each intersection of a given row and column—appear three pieces of information. The top number is the correlation coefficient itself; the number below this is the two-tailed *p*-value for the correlation; and the bottom number is the sample size (*N*) on which the correlation is based. Looking at the extreme upper-right corner, for example, we see that the correlation between *exercise* and *iq* equals .524, that *p* = .003, and that this is based on 30 cases (subjects). Thus, this correlation is significantly different from zero according to a two-tailed test at either the .05 or .01 alpha level. (If we had selected the "Flag significant correlations" option, then an asterisk would appear next to each correlation with a "Sig." value less than .05.)

Notice the redundancy in the table: Each correlation appears twice in the square matrix, as the upper-right triangle is a mirror image of the lower-left triangle. The same information about the *exercise–iq* correlation is printed in the extreme lower-left corner as well.

# Chapter 15

# Simple Regression

## Sample Problem

A second-grade teacher at Lakewood Elementary School believes that the amount of time parents spend reading to or with their children is a fairly accurate predictor of overall school performance. To test this hypothesis, the teacher conducted a study using the 25 students in his second-grade class. At the end of the school year, each child's letter grades for the entire year were used to calculate an overall grade-point average. During a PTA meeting, parents were given a questionnaire on which they were asked to indicate the average amount of time per week (in hours) that they spend reading to or with their children. (To avoid experimenter bias, the teacher did not look at the questionnaires until after he graded and calculated the grade-point averages for his students.) The results are listed as follows:

| Child | Reading Time (X) | GPA (Y) | Child | Reading Time (X) | GPA (Y) |
|-------|------------------|---------|-------|------------------|---------|
| 1     | 2   | 2.12 |    |    |      |
| 2     | 5   | 3.00 | 14 | 2  | 2.22 |
| 3     | 15  | 4.00 | 15 | 7  | 3.50 |
| 4     | 1   | 2.00 | 16 | 0  | 1.68 |
| 5     | 3   | 2.56 | 17 | 14 | 4.00 |
| 6     | 0   | 1.73 | 18 | 7  | 3.86 |
| 7     | 7   | 3.91 | 19 | 9  | 4.00 |
| 8     | 12  | 3.77 | 20 | 1  | 1.84 |
| 9     | 2   | 2.12 | 21 | 5  | 3.50 |
| 10    | 6   | 3.55 | 22 | 7  | 3.70 |
| 11    | 10  | 3.85 | 23 | 4  | 3.33 |
| 12    | 8   | 3.12 | 24 | 10 | 3.88 |
| 13    | 5   | 3.68 | 25 | 3  | 2.98 |

In this example, we wish to (1) find the equation that best represents the linear relationship between variables $X$ and $Y$ and that allows us to best predict $Y$ scores (GPA) from $X$ scores (reading time); (2) determine the strength of this relationship; and (3) test the null hypothesis that, in the population from which the sample was drawn, the slope of the prediction line is zero (that is, $X$ scores and $Y$ scores are unrelated).

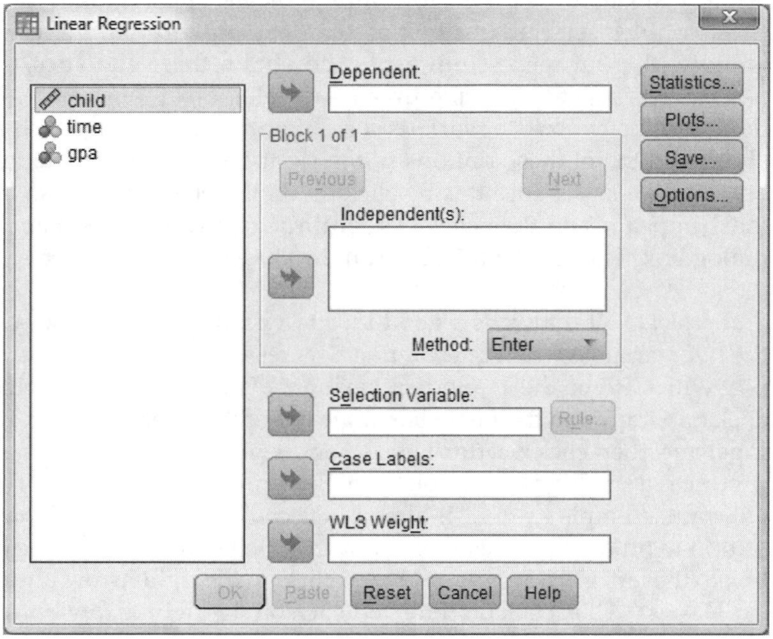

**Figure 15.1**

## Analysis

Following the procedure outlined in Chapter 2, enter the data into the first three columns of the Data Editor and label the variables **child**, **time**, and **gpa**.

Point-and-Click Method

Click on **Analyze** on the menu bar, and then choose **Regression**. From the resulting menu, choose **Linear . . . .** This produces a dialog box that looks like Figure 15.1.

The rest of the procedure is quite straightforward. As in previous procedures, choose the variables you wish to include in the analyses by moving them, one by one, from the box in which they appear on the left to either the "Dependent" box or the "Independent(s)" box on the right. In the present example, *gpa* is the dependent variable, so click on **gpa** in the left box and then on the right-arrow button pointing to the "Dependent" box. Our independent variable is **time**, so click on it (in the left box) and then click on the right-arrow button pointing to the "Independent(s)" box.

At this point, you may click on **OK** to run the analysis, or proceed one additional step to ask SPSS to print the means and standard deviations for the variables selected, as well as the Pearson correlation between them, along with your regression results. To obtain these statistics, click on the **Statistics . . .** button to bring up a new dialog box (not shown). This dialog box contains two lists of various sorts of options, some of which are already checked. One of these options in the right-hand column is labeled simply "Descriptives." Choose this by clicking on the box to its left so that a check mark appears, and then click on **Continue** to return to the main Regression dialog box. Then click on **OK** to run the analysis.

*Scatterplots.*   It is always a good idea to visually examine the scatterplot of the two variables when interpreting a regression analysis. To obtain a scatterplot with GPA on the *Y*- (vertical) axis and TIME on the *X*- (horizontal) axis, click on **Graphs** on the menu bar at the top of the screen, then on **Legacy Dialogs,** and then click **Scatter/Dot . . .** on the resulting pull-down menu. This produces a small dialog box picturing five kinds of scatterplots. The plot type we want, "Simple scatter," is already selected by default. Click on the **Define** button to produce another dialog box in which your variables are listed in the box to the left. Click on **gpa**, and then click on the right-arrow button pointing to "Y Axis." Then click on **time** and click on the right-arrow button pointing to "X Axis." Then click on **OK** to generate the scatterplot.

### Syntax Method

Open the Syntax Editor, type the following command (don't forget the period at the end!), and then click on the *Run* button to execute the analysis. (Note that we have used multiple lines and indentation for clarity, but this is optional.)

```
REGRESSION /DESCRIPTIVES
           /DEPENDENT = GPA
           /METHOD = ENTER TIME.
```

The **REGRESSION** command is used to produce both simple and multiple regression equations and associated statistics. Multiple regression, in which multiple predictor variables are used simultaneously, is covered in the next section of the manual.

The **/DESCRIPTIVES** subcommand tells SPSS to produce descriptive statistics for all the variables included in the analysis. These statistics include means, standard deviations, and a correlation matrix. This subcommand is optional, but we recommend it.

The **/DEPENDENT** subcommand is used to identify the dependent variable in the regression equation. In this example, our dependent variable is **GPA**.

The /**METHOD** subcommand must immediately follow the /**DEPEN-DENT** subcommand. The /**METHOD** subcommand is used to tell SPSS the way you want your independent variable(s) to be added to the regression equation. **ENTER** is the most direct method used to build a regression equation; it tells SPSS simply to enter all the independent variable(s) that you indicate for inclusion in the regression equation. In this example, we have only one independent variable, **TIME**, and of course we want it entered. Alternatives to **ENTER** will be discussed in the next chapter, on multiple regression.

*Scatterplots.* It is always a good idea to visually examine the scatterplot of the two variables when interpreting a regression analysis. A particularly useful kind of scatterplot is available via the Syntax Method that cannot be produced in the Point-and-Click Method. To create a scatterplot corresponding to the preceding analysis, simply use the following command instead of, or in addition to, the previous **REGRESSION** command:

```
GRAPH /SCATTERPLOT (BIVAR) = TIME WITH GPA.
```

This command requests a bivariate (two-variable) scatterplot, on which *time* will appear on the X- (horizontal) axis and *gpa* on the Y- (vertical) axis.

## Output

The output produced by SPSS for the sample problem, including the optional descriptive statistics, is shown in Figure 15.2.

If you requested descriptive statistics, these are printed first. The means, standard deviations, number of cases, and a correlation matrix are produced for the two variables *gpa* and *time.* The correlation between these two variables is .860, which indicates a strong, positive relationship; children whose parents spend more time reading to or with them tend to perform better in school.

Following the brief section titled "Variables Entered/Removed," SPSS produces regression statistics, including the multiple correlation coefficient ("R"), $R^2$ ("R Square"), adjusted or shrunken $R^2$ ("Adjusted R Square"), and the standard error of the estimate. Note that in simple regression, in which only one predictor variable is used, the multiple $R$ is equivalent to the simple correlation between the predictor and dependent variables—in this case, .860. Multiple $R^2$ represents the proportion of variance in the dependent variable predictable from the independent variable(s) (in this case, there is only one independent variable).

An ANOVA table for the regression equation is produced next; this represents a test of the null hypothesis that $R^2$ in the population equals zero. The variance of the dependent variable is partitioned into two sources: the

# Regression

**Descriptive Statistics**

|  | Mean | Std. Deviation | N |
|---|---|---|---|
| gpa | 3.1160 | .82289 | 25 |
| time | 5.80 | 4.203 | 25 |

**Correlations**

|  |  | gpa | time |
|---|---|---|---|
| Pearson Correlation | gpa | 1.000 | .860 |
|  | time | .860 | 1.000 |
| Sig. (1-tailed) | gpa | . | .000 |
|  | time | .000 | . |
| N | gpa | 25 | 25 |
|  | time | 25 | 25 |

**Variables Entered/Removed[b]**

| Model | Variables Entered | Variables Removed | Method |
|---|---|---|---|
| 1 | time[a] | . | Enter |

a. All requested variables entered.

b. Dependent Variable: gpa

**Model Summary**

| Model | R | R Square | Adjusted R Square | Std. Error of the Estimate |
|---|---|---|---|---|
| 1 | .860[a] | .739 | .728 | .42926 |

a. Predictors: (Constant), time

**ANOVA[b]**

| Model |  | Sum of Squares | df | Mean Square | F | Sig. |
|---|---|---|---|---|---|---|
| 1 | Regression | 12.013 | 1 | 12.013 | 65.198 | .000[a] |
|  | Residual | 4.238 | 23 | .184 |  |  |
|  | Total | 16.251 | 24 |  |  |  |

a. Predictors: (Constant), time

b. Dependent Variable: gpa

**Coefficients[a]**

| Model |  | Unstandardized Coefficients | | Standardized Coefficients | t | Sig. |
|---|---|---|---|---|---|---|
|  |  | B | Std. Error | Beta |  |  |
| 1 | (Constant) | 2.140 | .148 |  | 14.429 | .000 |
|  | time | .168 | .021 | .860 | 8.075 | .000 |

a. Dependent Variable: gpa

Figure 15.2

part predictable from the regression equation ("Regression") and the part not predictable from the equation ("Residual," or error). The *F*-test is significant. Two interesting things to note here are that (1) the sum of squares due to regression divided by the sum of squares total (that is, regression plus residual) equals $R^2$—this is the proportion of variance in the dependent variable that is predictable from the independent variable; and (2) the significance test for $R^2$, when there is only one predictor variable, is equivalent to a simple test of the correlation between the independent and dependent variables.

The final section of the output provides the information needed to construct a least-squares regression (prediction) equation. The column labeled "B" lists the regression coefficients for the independent variable *time* and for the "Constant" term. These represent the slope and *Y*-intercept, respectively, for the regression line and are usually represented as $b_1$ and $b_0$. Thus, in this example, the least-squares prediction equation is:

Predicted GPA = 2.140 + (.168)*(TIME)

The values listed under "Beta" represent an alternative set of coefficients that would be used instead if all variables were first converted to Z-scores— that is, if they were first standardized. Note that there is no value for "Constant" in this column. If both variables are in Z-score form, the *Y*-intercept is always zero. Thus, the prediction equation for predicting Z-scores on *Y* from Z-scores on *X* is:

Predicted $Z_{GPA}$ = 0 + (.860)*($Z_{TIME}$)

or more simply:

Predicted $Z_{GPA}$ = (.860)*($Z_{TIME}$)

The last two columns report the results of the significance tests for the coefficients. The null hypothesis being tested on each line is that the particular *b* coefficient (or the beta coefficient—the tests are equivalent) equals zero in the population. The *t*- and *p*-values for these tests are labeled "t" and "Sig.," respectively. Both *p*-values are reported as ".000," which in this case means that the actual *p*-values are less than .0005 and are rounded off. Both coefficients (the slope $b_1$ and the intercept $b_0$) are significantly different from zero.

*Scatterplots.*   Figure 15.3 shows a scatterplot of variables *gpa* and *time*. Each point represents a research subject: The vertical location of the point represents the subject's score on *gpa,* and the horizontal location represents his or her score on *time*.

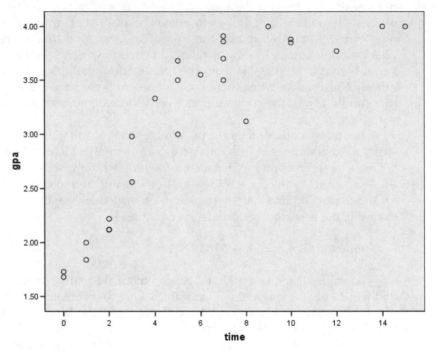

**Figure 15.3**

# Chapter 16

# Multiple Regression

## Sample Problem

A resilience researcher conducted a study with an at-risk preschool population in a continuing effort to determine why many children growing up in potentially damaging environments come through relatively unharmed and well adjusted whereas other children succumb to the stress. This preschool population was deemed to be at risk for educational and developmental delays due to a number of risk factors, including low social status, parental psychiatric disorders or criminality, and overcrowding/large family size. Because past resilience research suggested that family social support, child biological dispositions (temperament), and characteristics of the home environment are associated with the likelihood of future adaptive outcomes, the researcher decided to investigate these variables to determine whether they would be powerful predictors of resilience in a sample of 30 at-risk preschool children. The children were tested for age-appropriate developmental abilities (verbal, motor, cognitive, self-help, emotional, and social), and an aggregate score for these abilities was used as the dependent measure of resilience. (Higher scores indicate greater overall developmental abilities.) Families were asked to fill out a social support questionnaire to measure the helpfulness of sources of support to families raising a young child. (Higher scores indicate greater support.) Teachers were asked to rate aspects of each child's home environment (such as emotional and verbal responsiveness of parents, learning and language stimulation, availability of play materials, and so on) during regular home visits. (Higher scores indicate a more positive home environment.) A child temperament scale was also completed by teachers. (Higher scores indicate an easy, adaptive, flexible temperamental style, and lower scores indicate an intense, difficult, less malleable temperamental style.) The results are as follows:

| Child | Social Support | Temperament | Home Environment | Development |
|-------|----------------|-------------|------------------|-------------|
| 1  | 37 | 21 | 20 | 25 |
| 2  | 85 | 38 | 25 | 48 |
| 3  | 43 | 18 | 19 | 22 |
| 4  | 68 | 37 | 27 | 49 |
| 5  | 30 | 12 | 18 | 15 |
| 6  | 57 | 33 | 23 | 37 |
| 7  | 87 | 38 | 29 | 60 |
| 8  | 15 | 35 | 22 | 30 |
| 9  | 72 | 41 | 36 | 55 |
| 10 | 40 | 35 | 21 | 27 |
| 11 | 60 | 34 | 20 | 47 |

| Child | Social Support | Temperament | Home Environment | Development |
|-------|----------------|-------------|------------------|------------|
| 12 | 54 | 29 | 26 | 43 |
| 13 | 79 | 31 | 35 | 50 |
| 14 | 56 | 32 | 28 | 45 |
| 15 | 35 | 25 | 29 | 27 |
| 16 | 53 | 28 | 24 | 39 |
| 17 | 75 | 39 | 31 | 52 |
| 18 | 70 | 35 | 26 | 53 |
| 19 | 79 | 31 | 24 | 60 |
| 20 | 31 | 42 | 19 | 20 |
| 21 | 17 | 40 | 22 | 32 |
| 22 | 82 | 41 | 31 | 58 |
| 23 | 59 | 40 | 27 | 41 |
| 24 | 26 | 25 | 15 | 17 |
| 25 | 54 | 39 | 24 | 33 |
| 26 | 27 | 19 | 19 | 20 |
| 27 | 62 | 45 | 29 | 44 |
| 28 | 79 | 47 | 28 | 56 |
| 29 | 26 | 30 | 10 | 18 |
| 30 | 69 | 33 | 29 | 59 |

In multiple regression, a dependent variable (in this case, *developmental ability*) is predicted from several independent variables simultaneously. As in simple regression, however, we are interested in determining (1) the equation for best predicting the dependent variable from a linear combination of predictors, and (2) how well this "best" equation does in fact predict variability in the dependent variable. In addition, we usually are interested in significance tests to assess the contributions of each of the variables to the prediction equation.

A popular but controversial variation on multiple regression analysis involves what are known as "stepwise" selection methods. In these procedures, the user provides a list of potential independent variables and allows the program to choose among them based on statistical criteria. Such procedures result in a series of regression analyses in which independent variables are systematically added or subtracted from the equation one by one and a new regression equation computed at each step until some predetermined statistical criterion is reached. We do not believe these procedures are to be recommended for most purposes, and in our example we show simply how to compute the multiple regression equation for a single set of predictor variables selected by the user. However, we note in passing how to conduct stepwise analyses for those who wish to do so.

One of the most important uses of multiple regression involves comparing two hierarchical models (that is, the predictor variables in one represent a subset of the predictor variables in the other) against each other. In the present example, for instance, you might want to test the "full" model containing all three predictors with a "reduced" model containing only, say, *temperament*;

this comparison would test the hypothesis that *social support* and *home environment*, collectively, predict additional variance in the dependent variable above and beyond what can be predicted by *temperament* alone. In a final section, we discuss how to conduct such model-comparison tests.

## Analysis

Following the procedure outlined in Chapter 2, enter the data into the first five columns of the Data Editor and label the variables **subject**, **support**, **temper**, **homeenv**, and **develop**.

### Point-and-Click Method

Follow the procedures outlined in the previous chapter on simple regression. Click on **Analyze** on the menu bar, and then choose **Regression**. From the resulting menu, choose **Linear . . . .** In the resulting dialog box (similar to Figure 15.1 in the previous chapter, but, of course, with different variable names listed in the left-hand box), move the variable **develop** into the "Dependent" box and move the variables **support**, **temper**, and **homeenv** into the "Independent(s)" box. To get descriptive statistics (including correlations), click on the **Statistics . . .** button and select "Descriptives" in the resulting dialog box. Click on **Continue** to close this dialog box, then on **OK** to run the analysis.

*Stepwise Variable Selection.* To run one of the so-called stepwise procedures, complete the preceding steps for all of the potential independent variables of interest in the "Independent(s)" box. Near the middle of the dialog box you'll see the word "Method," and to the right of this, the word "Enter" appears in a small box. To the right of this, in turn, is a small downward-pointing arrow button. Click on this button to produce a pull-down menu that lists several options. Simply click on **Stepwise, Backward,** or **Forward** to choose one of these stepwise methods; then click on **OK** to run the analysis.

*Model Comparisons.* Specification of a comparison between two hierarchical models, as in the example described near the beginning of this chapter, requires two steps, which can be done in either of two ways. One way is to begin by specifying the "full" (larger) model, exactly as described previously in this chapter. For the present example, choose the dependent variable **develop** and all three independent (predictor) variables. However, before clicking on **OK**, click on the button labeled **Next**, which is between the "Dependent" and "Independent(s)" boxes (see Figure 15.1). The text to the left of this button will change to say "Block 2 of 2," to indicate that you are now going to specify the second step, and the list of "Independent(s)" will be empty again. Now move the variables **support** and **homeenv** (but not **temper**) from the left box into the "Independent(s)" box. Click on the downward-pointing arrow next to "Method: Enter," and choose **Remove** from the pull-down menu. Finally, click on the **Statistics . . .** button (at the right in the dialog box), and in the resulting screen, choose the option labeled "R squared change." This important last step asks SPSS to print the results of the crucial test assessing whether the "full," three-predictor model predicts significantly more variance in the dependent variable than does the "reduced" model (from which two predictors were removed). Click on **Continue** to close this dialog box, and then click on **OK** to run the analysis.

The alternative way of conducting this test is essentially the reverse of the first: Instead of beginning with a "full" model and then removing two predictors from it, you begin with the "reduced" model and then ask SPSS to *add* the other predictors at the second step. The procedure follows the same basic steps as in the preceding paragraph: (1) First specify the one-predictor (**temper**) model; (2) click on **Next**; (3) move **support** and **homeenv** to the "Independent(s)" list; (4) change "Method" to **Enter** (rather than **Remove**, as in the preceding paragraph); (5) click on **Statistics . . .** and choose "R squared change"; and (6) click **Continue**, then **OK**.

Whichever of these ways you choose, each section in the resulting output will have separate lines corresponding to "Model 1" and "Model 2"; a section at the beginning of the output will remind you what variables were entered or removed at each step. The section of the output containing the crucial significance test comparing the models is reproduced later in this chapter (see Figure 16.2).

## Syntax Method

Open the Syntax Editor, type the following command (don't forget the period at the end!), and then click on the *Run* button to execute the analysis. (Note that we have used multiple lines and indentation for clarity, but this is optional.)

```
REGRESSION /VARIABLES = SUPPORT TEMPER HOMEENV DEVELOP
           /DESCRIPTIVES
           /DEPENDENT = DEVELOP
           /METHOD = ENTER SUPPORT TEMPER HOMEENV.
```

The **REGRESSION** command is used to produce multiple regression equations and associated statistics.

The **/VARIABLES** subcommand is used to specify the names of all the variables (dependent and independent) that we will be using in the analysis. (Note that this subcommand is optional because, if omitted, SPSS produces regression equations and statistics for the variables named on the **/DEPENDENT** and **/METHOD** subcommands by default. Also, because we did name all of our variables on the **/VARIABLES** subcommand, we could have simply typed the word **ENTER** after the **/METHOD** subcommand without specifying any independent variable names. In this case, SPSS enters all the variables listed on the **/VARIABLES** subcommand except the dependent variable.) The variables that we are using in this analysis are **SUPPORT, TEMPER, HOMEENV,** and **DEVELOP.**

The **/DESCRIPTIVES** subcommand tells SPSS to produce descriptive statistics for all the variables included in the analysis. These statistics include means, standard deviations, and a correlation matrix.

The **/DEPENDENT** subcommand is used to identify the dependent variable in the regression equation. In this example, the dependent variable is **DEVELOP.**

The **/METHOD** subcommand must immediately follow the **/DEPEN-DENT** subcommand. The **/METHOD** subcommand is used to tell SPSS the way you want your independent variable(s) to be added to the regression equation. **ENTER** is the most direct method used to build a regression equation; it tells SPSS to enter all the independent variable(s) (in a single step) that you indicate for inclusion in the regression equation. In this example, the independent variables are **SUPPORT, TEMPER,** and **HOMEENV.**

*Stepwise Variable Selection.*   To run one of the various stepwise procedures, replace the word **ENTER** on the **METHOD** line with one of the following: **FORWARD, BACKWARD, STEPWISE.**

*Model Comparisons.*   Specification of a comparison between two hierarchical models, as in the example described near the beginning of this chapter, requires two steps, which can be done in either of two ways. One way is to specify the "full" (larger) model, exactly as described previously, and then to specify that one or more variables be removed from the model. The syntax for this example is as follows:

```
REGRESSION /STATISTICS COEFF OUTS R ANOVA CHANGE
           /DEPENDENT = DEVELOP
           /METHOD = ENTER SUPPORT TEMPER HOMEENV
           /METHOD = REMOVE SUPPORT HOMEENV.
```

Note that a **/STATISTICS** subcommand is now required. This was not important previously because all of the statistics we were interested in were produced by SPSS by default. However, the crucial test for comparing the two models is not printed by SPSS unless we ask for it specifically. The **/STATISTICS** subcommand, therefore, requests all the statistics that are normally produced by default, plus this crucial extra test (**CHANGE**).

An alternative way to accomplish the same thing is to specify the smaller ("reduced") model in the first **/METHOD** statement, and then add a second **/METHOD** statement that tells SPSS which additional variables to then **ENTER** to construct the second model. In the present example, the syntax would be:

```
REGRESSION /STATISTICS COEFF OUTS R ANOVA CHANGE
            /DEPENDENT = DEVELOP
            /METHOD = ENTER TEMPER
            /METHOD = ENTER SUPPORT HOMEENV.
```

Whichever of these ways you choose, each section in the resulting output will have separate lines corresponding to "Model 1" and "Model 2"; a section at the beginning of the output will remind you what variables were entered or removed at each step. The section of the output containing the crucial significance test comparing the models is reproduced later in this chapter.

## Output

The output produced by SPSS for the sample problem, including the optional descriptive statistics, is shown in Figure 16.1.

If you requested descriptive statistics, the means, standard deviations, number of cases, and a correlation matrix are produced for all the variables (both dependent and independent) used in the analysis. In this example, all independent variables correlate positively with the dependent variable. (In some versions, two additional matrices are also printed along with the correlations: a matrix of one-tailed $p$-values labeled "Sig." and a matrix of sample sizes labeled "N.")

Following a brief section ("Variables Entered/Removed") confirming your analysis specification, SPSS produces regression statistics, including the multiple correlation coefficient ("R"), $R^2$ ("R Square"), adjusted or shrunken $R^2$ ("Adjusted R Square"), and the standard error of the estimate. Unlike simple regression, in which only one predictor variable is used, the multiple $R$ is not equivalent to any of the simple pairwise correlations printed previously. Multiple $R$ represents the correlation between actual scores on the dependent variable and predicted scores based on the regression equation. Multiple $R^2$, the square of this, represents the proportion of variance predictable in the dependent variable from the regression equation.

An ANOVA table for the regression equation is produced next; this represents a test of the null hypothesis that multiple $R$ (and $R^2$) in the population equals zero. The variance of the dependent variable is partitioned into two sources: the part predictable from the regression equation ("Regression") and the part not predictable from the equation ("Residual," or error). In this example, the $F$-test is significant. As in simple regression, the sum of squares regression divided by the sum of squares total (that is, regression plus residual) equals $R^2$.

The final section of the output provides the information needed to construct a least-squares regression (prediction) equation. The column labeled "B" lists the regression coefficients for each independent variable and for the "Constant" term. Thus, in this example, the least-squares prediction equation is:

# Regression

## Descriptive Statistics

|        | Mean  | Std. Deviation | N  |
|--------|-------|----------------|----|
| develop | 39.40 | 14.576 | 30 |
| support | 54.23 | 21.614 | 30 |
| temper  | 33.10 | 8.285  | 30 |
| homeenv | 24.53 | 5.728  | 30 |

## Correlations

|                       |         | develop | support | temper | homeenv |
|-----------------------|---------|---------|---------|--------|---------|
| Pearson Correlation   | develop | 1.000   | .899    | .582   | .776    |
|                       | support | .899    | 1.000   | .468   | .716    |
|                       | temper  | .582    | .468    | 1.000  | .481    |
|                       | homeenv | .776    | .716    | .481   | 1.000   |
| Sig. (1-tailed)       | develop | .       | .000    | .000   | .000    |
|                       | support | .000    | .       | .005   | .000    |
|                       | temper  | .000    | .005    | .      | .004    |
|                       | homeenv | .000    | .000    | .004   | .       |
| N                     | develop | 30      | 30      | 30     | 30      |
|                       | support | 30      | 30      | 30     | 30      |
|                       | temper  | 30      | 30      | 30     | 30      |
|                       | homeenv | 30      | 30      | 30     | 30      |

## Variables Entered/Removed[b]

| Model | Variables Entered | Variables Removed | Method |
|-------|-------------------|-------------------|--------|
| 1 | homeenv, temper,[a] support | . | Enter |

a. All requested variables entered.

b. Dependent Variable: develop

## Model Summary

| Model | R | R Square | Adjusted R Square | Std. Error of the Estimate |
|-------|------|----------|-------------------|----------------------------|
| 1 | .930[a] | .865 | .849 | 5.664 |

a. Predictors: (Constant), homeenv, temper, support

**Figure 16.1**

*(continued on next page)*

**ANOVA<sup>b</sup>**

| Model | | Sum of Squares | df | Mean Square | F | Sig. |
|---|---|---|---|---|---|---|
| 1 | Regression | 5326.979 | 3 | 1775.660 | 55.342 | .000<sup>a</sup> |
| | Residual | 834.221 | 26 | 32.085 | | |
| | Total | 6161.200 | 29 | | | |

a. Predictors: (Constant), homeenv, temper, support

b. Dependent Variable: develop

**Coefficients<sup>a</sup>**

| Model | | Unstandardized Coefficients | | Standardized Coefficients | t | Sig. |
|---|---|---|---|---|---|---|
| | | B | Std. Error | Beta | | |
| 1 | (Constant) | -8.307 | 5.344 | | -1.555 | .132 |
| | support | .447 | .071 | .663 | 6.284 | .000 |
| | temper | .291 | .148 | .165 | 1.967 | .060 |
| | homeenv | .563 | .271 | .221 | 2.080 | .048 |

a. Dependent Variable: develop

**Figure 16.1** *(continued)*

Predicted DEVELOP $= -8.307 + (.563)*(HOMEENV) + (.291)*(TEMPER) + (.447)*(SUPPORT)$

The values listed under "Beta" represent an alternative set of coefficients that would be used instead if all variables were first converted to Z-scores—that is, if they were first standardized. Note that there is no value for "Constant" in this column. If all variables are in Z-score form, the Y-intercept is always zero. Thus, the prediction equation for predicting Z-scores on Y from Z-scores on the various predictors is:

Predicted $Z_{DEVELOP} = 0 + (.221)*(Z_{HOMEENV}) + (.165)*(Z_{TEMPER}) + (.663)*(Z_{SUPPORT})$

The last two columns report the results of the significance tests for the coefficients. The null hypotheses being tested are, in each case, that the *b* coefficient in question equals zero in the population. In this case, the tests for *homeenv* and *support* are significant at the .05 level, but the test for *temper* is not significant.

### Stepwise Variable Selection

If you chose one of the stepwise methods of variable selection, your output will generally contain the results of several multiple regressions, in which each successive analysis adds or deletes one independent variable relative to the previous one. The final analysis reported is the one ultimately chosen by SPSS as the "best" equation as defined by that particular stepwise procedure.

### Model Comparisons

If you specified a model comparison using the first procedure we discussed—that is, by specifying the "full" three-predictor model and then removing two variables from it—the crucial part of your output will look like Figure 16.2. The last part of the "Model Summary" contains the crucial test comparing the two models. The line for Model 1 gives $R^2$ (.865) for the three-predictor model and an $F$-test for the hypothesis that $R^2$ in the population equals zero. This test is significant and is identical to the one in Figure 16.1. The line for Model 2 then shows the *change* in $R^2$ (−.526) when the predictor variables *support* and *homeenv* are removed. The $F$-test on this line tests the hypothesis that this change in $R^2$ equals zero in the population—that is, the hypothesis that removing *support* and *homeenv* has no effect on prediction. The significant result here suggests that *support* and *homeenv* do, in fact, collectively add to prediction above and beyond what can be predicted by *temper* alone.

Had we used the alternative procedure, in which Model 1 included only one predictor and Model 2 added the two other predictors, the change in $R^2$ reported on the Model 2 line would have been a positive rather than a negative .526, but the corresponding $F$-test result would have been identical.

# Regression

**Variables Entered/Removed[c]**

| Model | Variables Entered | Variables Removed | Method |
|---|---|---|---|
| 1 | homeenv, temper, support [a] | | Enter |
| 2 | | homeenv, support [b] | Remove |

a. All requested variables entered.

b. All requested variables removed.

c. Dependent Variable: develop

**Model Summary**

| Model | R | R Square | Adjusted R Square | Std. Error of the Estimate | Change Statistics | | | | |
|---|---|---|---|---|---|---|---|---|---|
| | | | | | R Square Change | F Change | df1 | df2 | Sig. F Change |
| 1 | .930[a] | .865 | .849 | 5.664 | .865 | 55.342 | 3 | 26 | .000 |
| 2 | .582[b] | .339 | .315 | 12.061 | -.526 | 50.473 | 2 | 26 | .000 |

a. Predictors: (Constant), homeenv, temper, support

b. Predictors: (Constant), temper

**Figure 16.2**

# Chapter 17

# Chi-Square Test of Independence

## Sample Problem

A psychology student intern, who was volunteering at a nursing home to fulfill a requirement for her psychology of aging course, noticed that there seemed to be a relationship between how frequently a patient received visitors and how well a patient was treated by the nursing home staff. Therefore, the student decided to test whether there is significant evidence to conclude that frequency of visitors and staff treatment of patients are related. The student used the visitor log book to determine the frequency of visitors for a random sample of 39 patients. She categorized each patient into one of three visitor categories: frequently visited, occasionally visited, or rarely/never visited. She then asked a nursing intern (who was blind to the purpose of the study) to rate (based on conversations with the patients and personal observations) how well she thought each patient was being treated by the nursing home staff. Each patient was categorized into one of three treatment categories: excellent/good treatment, fair treatment, or poor treatment. The results are as follows (for visitors, 1 = frequent, 2 = occasional, 3 = rarely/never; for treatment, 1 = excellent/good, 2 = fair, 3 = poor):

| Patient | Visitors | Treatment |
|---------|----------|-----------|
| 1 | 1 | 1 |
| 2 | 1 | 1 |
| 3 | 1 | 1 |
| 4 | 1 | 1 |
| 5 | 1 | 1 |
| 6 | 1 | 1 |
| 7 | 1 | 1 |
| 8 | 1 | 1 |
| 9 | 1 | 1 |
| 10 | 1 | 2 |
| 11 | 1 | 2 |
| 12 | 1 | 2 |
| 13 | 1 | 3 |
| 14 | 2 | 1 |
| 15 | 2 | 2 |
| 16 | 2 | 2 |
| 17 | 2 | 2 |
| 18 | 2 | 2 |
| 19 | 2 | 2 |
| 20 | 2 | 2 |

| Patient | Visitors | Treatment |
|---------|----------|-----------|
| 21 | 2 | 2 |
| 22 | 2 | 2 |
| 23 | 2 | 2 |
| 24 | 2 | 2 |
| 25 | 2 | 3 |
| 26 | 2 | 3 |
| 27 | 3 | 1 |
| 28 | 3 | 2 |
| 29 | 3 | 3 |
| 30 | 3 | 3 |
| 31 | 3 | 3 |
| 32 | 3 | 3 |
| 33 | 3 | 3 |
| 34 | 3 | 3 |
| 35 | 3 | 3 |
| 36 | 3 | 3 |
| 37 | 3 | 3 |
| 38 | 3 | 3 |
| 39 | 3 | 3 |

In this problem, we are testing the null hypothesis that the frequency of visitors that patients receive and treatment of patients by nursing home staff are independent. In other words, there is no relationship between how frequently a patient receives visitors and how well a patient is treated by the nursing home staff.

## Analysis

Following the procedure outlined in Chapter 2, enter the data into the first three columns of the Data Editor and label the variables **patient**, **visitors**, and **treat**.

### Point-and-Click Method

To obtain a cross-tabulation table and chi-square test of association, click on **Analyze**, and then choose **Descriptive Statistics** from the pull-down menu. Then click on **Crosstabs . . .** to produce the dialog box illustrated in Figure 17.1.

As in many other procedures, your variable list appears in a box to the left, and you need to move the names of the variables you wish to analyze into the appropriate boxes on the right. Click on **visitors** in the left box, then on the right-arrow button to move this variable to the box labeled "Row(s)." Then click on **treat** and move it to the "Column(s)" box by clicking on the appropriate right-arrow button. (Note that the choice of row versus column variables is arbitrary; you could just as easily have made **treat** the row variable and **visitors** the column variable.) Don't click **OK** just yet.

Now click on the **Cells . . .** button at the upper right in the dialog box. This produces a new dialog box (not shown) in which you may specify the kinds of information you would like printed in each cell (that is, each **visitors × treat** combination) of the cross-tabulation table. By default, each cell of the table contains only the number of cases for that particular cell—this is labeled **Observed**. Choosing **Expected** tells SPSS to print also the expected frequencies for each cell—that is, the number of cases expected in each cell if the row variable and the column variable were independent (the "E" values in the chi-square formula). Choosing **Row** (under "Percentages") asks SPSS to print percentages relative to the number of cases per row, and choosing **Column** does likewise relative to columns. We have selected all of these in this example. Click on **Continue** when you are finished.

There is still one more step. To request a chi-square test or other statistical analysis, click on **Statistics . . .** at the right in the main "Crosstabs" dialog box. This produces a dialog box containing a list of different statistical analyses, many of which are probably unfamiliar. You may choose as many of these as you wish, but for present purposes we need select only "Chi-square." (One other important statistic available here is *kappa*, which

**Figure 17.1**

produces a measure of strength of association for symmetrical tables that is commonly used for assessing inter-rater reliability.) Then click on **Continue** to return to the main "Crosstabs" dialog box, and click on **OK** to run the analysis.

Syntax Method

Open the Syntax Editor, type the following command (don't forget the period at the end!), and then click on the *Run* button to execute the analysis. (Note that we have used multiple lines and indentation for clarity, but this is optional.)

```
CROSSTABS /TABLES = VISITORS BY TREAT
         /CELLS = COUNT EXPECTED ROW COLUMN
         /STATISTICS = CHISQ.
```

The **CROSSTABS** command is used to compute cross-tabulations and various measures of association for two or more variables.

The subcommand **/TABLES** is used to specify the cross-tabulation table(s) that you want SPSS to produce. After typing **/TABLES**, you must type the name of your row variable. In this example, the row variable is **VISITORS**. Each level of the variable **VISITORS** defines one row of the table (1 = frequent; 2 = occasional; 3 = rarely/never). Then, you must type the word **BY**, followed by the name of your column variable. In this example, the column variable is **TREAT** (for "treatment"). Each level of the variable **TREAT** defines one column of the table (1 = excellent/good; 2 = fair; 3 = poor). Note that the word **BY** distinguishes row variables from column variables. If you typed more than one row and column variable, SPSS would produce a table for every possible pair of a row variable with a column variable.

By default, each cell of the table contains only the number of cases for that particular cell. The subcommand **/CELLS** is used to specify additional cell contents. **COUNT** confirms that you want SPSS to produce the number of cases for each cell—that is, the observed or "O" values used in the calculation of chi-square. **EXPECTED** tells SPSS to print also the expected frequencies for each cell—that is, the number of cases expected in each cell if the row variable and the column variable were independent (the "E" values in the chi-square formula). Other options that can be added include **ROW**, which calculates and prints percentages relative to number of cases per row; **COLUMN**, which does likewise relative to columns; and **TOTAL**, which reports each cell in terms of the percentage of the total number of cases in the table.

The subcommand **/STATISTICS = CHISQ** tells SPSS to produce the chi-square statistic, along with its associated degrees of freedom and significance level. Many other statistics are available in addition to or instead of **CHISQ**, but most will be familiar only to advanced users. (One other important statistic available here is **KAPPA**, which produces a measure of strength of association for symmetrical tables that is commonly used for assessing inter-rater reliability.)

## Output

The output produced by SPSS for the sample problem is shown in Figure 17.2.

The first table, the "Case Processing Summary," simply indicates the number of cases (patients, in this case) who are included in the cross-tabulation table. In this example, we had complete data for every patient, so there are 39 "valid" cases and no "missing" cases.

The cross-tabulation table in this example includes four pieces of information for each cell, as specified in our example. A legend explaining the contents of each cell appears at the left of each row. The top number in each cell is the observed frequency ("Count"), followed below by the expected frequency ("Expected Count"), row percentage (in this case, "%

# Crosstabs

## Case Processing Summary

| | Cases | | | | | |
|---|---|---|---|---|---|---|
| | Valid | | Missing | | Total | |
| | N | Percent | N | Percent | N | Percent |
| visitors * treat | 39 | 100.0% | 0 | .0% | 39 | 100.0% |

## visitors * treat Crosstabulation

| | | | treat | | | |
|---|---|---|---|---|---|---|
| | | | 1 | 2 | 3 | Total |
| visitors | 1 | Count | 9 | 3 | 1 | 13 |
| | | Expected Count | 3.7 | 4.7 | 4.7 | 13.0 |
| | | % within visitors | 69.2% | 23.1% | 7.7% | 100.0% |
| | | % within treat | 81.8% | 21.4% | 7.1% | 33.3% |
| | 2 | Count | 1 | 10 | 2 | 13 |
| | | Expected Count | 3.7 | 4.7 | 4.7 | 13.0 |
| | | % within visitors | 7.7% | 76.9% | 15.4% | 100.0% |
| | | % within treat | 9.1% | 71.4% | 14.3% | 33.3% |
| | 3 | Count | 1 | 1 | 11 | 13 |
| | | Expected Count | 3.7 | 4.7 | 4.7 | 13.0 |
| | | % within visitors | 7.7% | 7.7% | 84.6% | 100.0% |
| | | % within treat | 9.1% | 7.1% | 78.6% | 33.3% |
| Total | | Count | 11 | 14 | 14 | 39 |
| | | Expected Count | 11.0 | 14.0 | 14.0 | 39.0 |
| | | % within visitors | 28.2% | 35.9% | 35.9% | 100.0% |
| | | % within treat | 100.0% | 100.0% | 100.0% | 100.0% |

## Chi-Square Tests

| | Value | df | Asymp. Sig. (2-sided) |
|---|---|---|---|
| Pearson Chi-Square | 34.208[a] | 4 | .000 |
| Likelihood Ratio | 32.871 | 4 | .000 |
| Linear-by-Linear Association | 19.118 | 1 | .000 |
| N of Valid Cases | 39 | | |

a. 9 cells (100.0%) have expected count less than 5. The minimum expected count is 3.67.

Figure 17.2

within visitors"), and column percentage ("% within treat"). Thus, for example, nine patients were observed in the cell defined by *visitors* = 1 and *treat* = 1 (upper-left cell in the table). The expected frequency for this cell is 3.7, which could be found by hand by multiplying the number of patients in the *visitors* = 1 row (13) by the number of patients in the *treat* = 1 column (11) and dividing by the total number of patients in the table (39): 13*11/39 = 3.66666 (which SPSS has rounded off to 3.7). The row percentage (69.2%) means that the observed frequency in this cell (9) represents 69.2% of the 13 observations in the *visitors* = 1 row. Similarly, the column percentage (81.8%) indicates that the observed frequency of 9 represents 81.8% of the 11 observations in the *treat* = 1 column.

Next, several chi-square test statistics are produced, along with their associated degrees of freedom and significance levels. The chi-square statistic provides a test of the null hypothesis that the proportion of patients receiving excellent, fair, and poor treatment in nursing homes is the same for patients who receive frequent, occasional, and no visitors; in other words, that treatment quality is not related to visitation frequency. Of these chi-square statistics, the Pearson statistic is most commonly used for this purpose and is taught in most textbooks. In this case, the observed Pearson chi-square value equals 34.208, and there are 4 degrees of freedom (the product of the number of columns minus 1 and the number of rows minus 1). The associated *p*-value, labeled "Asymp. Sig. (2-sided)," is reported as .000, which means it is less than .0005 and was rounded off. There is a significant relationship between the two variables.

At the bottom of the output, SPSS prints out the number of cells whose expected frequencies are less than 5. (This can be easily confirmed by examining the table itself because we asked SPSS to print the expected frequencies for us in this example.) This number is given because some of the assumptions underlying the chi-square test are questionable in small samples, and statisticians commonly suggest a rule of thumb that *all* expected frequencies be at least 5 in order for the chi-square test to be considered reliable. In this particular example, all nine cells have expected values less than 5, suggesting that the results of the chi-square test must be interpreted with great caution.

# Saving and Retrieving Files

Before leaving SPSS for Windows, be sure to save any parts of your work that you might want to use again. Once you've typed all your data into the Data Editor, for example, you might want to save the data if you think you might want to do something else with those data later on. The main items you might want to save are the output produced by your analyses (from the Output Viewer), the data file (from the Data Editor), and (if you are using the Syntax Method) the SPSS program commands in the Syntax Editor.

## File Types

Saving and retrieving your work in SPSS involve many different types of files that contain different kinds of information, and it is important to keep track of the differences among them. The file types discussed in this book include *data* files, containing the data, variable names, and so forth as contained in the Data Editor; *output* files, containing the results of analyses as displayed in the Output Viewer; and *syntax* files (if you use the Syntax Method), containing SPSS program commands. These various types of files differ not only in the information they contain but also in the format in which they are saved by SPSS. It is as if they were stored in different languages, and as a result they are not interchangeable even if for some reason you wanted them to be. The Data Editor doesn't understand output files, the Output Viewer doesn't understand syntax files, and so forth.

Consequently, it is a good idea when saving files to give them names in a way that helps you immediately identify what type of file they represent. The conventional way of doing this (a legacy of MS-DOS) is by use of different *file extensions*. When naming a file, you have the option of adding to the end of the name a period (.) followed by three letters or numbers; this is the file extension. SPSS uses this convention by referring to all data files with the extension **.sav**; for example, you might save the data from Chapter 6 (involving students' scores on a midterm exam) under the file name **midterm.sav**. For syntax files, SPSS uses the extension **.sps**; thus the syntax you typed into the Syntax Editor in Chapter 6 (if you used the Syntax Method) might be saved under the file name **midterm.sps**. For output files, SPSS uses the extension **.spv**. Thus, if you save the output from the problem in Chapter 6 to a file, you might call the file **midterm.spv.** You will find it helpful to adopt these conventions yourself and to be careful about always naming your files in this way.

## Saving Files

The best way to save something into a file is to do it while the window whose contents you wish to save is the active window on your screen. You can move between windows by clicking at any time on **Window** on the menu bar at the top of the screen, and then choosing the desired window from the resulting pull-down menu. Then, once that window appears, you can save its contents by clicking on **File** on the menu bar, then **Save As** on the resulting pull-down menu. This produces a dialog box in which you specify the name you wish to give the file or folder.

To illustrate, suppose we have entered the data from Chapter 6 into the Data Editor, and, while viewing the Data Editor, we click on **File** on the menu bar and choose **Save As** from the resulting menu. This produces a dialog box similar to Figure A.1. Note that the dialog box is labeled "Save Data As"; it will be labeled differently (and appropriately) if you issue the **Save As** command while viewing syntax or output instead.

SPSS assumes that you want to save a file of type **.sav** (that is, a data file), and you should be sure to name the file using the **.sav** extension. Again, the

**Figure A.1**

file type will be different if you are saving a syntax file (**.sps**) or output file (**.spv**). The dialog boxes also indicate the default directory or folder in which, unless you tell SPSS otherwise, it will save the file. Finally, the box shows you a list of files in the default (folder) directory with the file extension of interest. Move to the folder or location where you wish to save the file, and type the file name you wish to use.

## Retrieving Files

The whole point of saving files is, of course, so you can retrieve them later to view or use them again. To do so, click on **File** on the menu bar and then on **Open . . .** from the resulting menu. This produces a list of types of files from which you must choose by clicking on **Data . . .** (or **Syntax . . .** , **Output . . .** , etc.). Selecting one of these opens a dialog box very similar to Figure A.1, except that (1) it is labeled "Open File," and (2) the box at the bottom, labeled "Save as type" in Figure A.1, is instead labeled "Files of type." The default type is that corresponding to the kind of window you were viewing when you issued the **Open . . .** command. Locate the file you wish to retrieve, and double-click on its name to open it.

If you instead had selected a syntax file—say, a file called **midterm. sps** containing the **FREQUENCIES** command syntax discussed in Chapter 6—you would immediately be placed into the Syntax Editor (rather than the Data Editor), which contains the syntax you had saved previously in this file. Likewise, selecting an output file places you into the Output Viewer, in which the previously saved output is displayed. Note that SPSS automatically detects the type of file and reads it into the appropriate window. Once you're there, you can do anything you would normally be able to do in that particular window, including editing or printing the contents, executing the syntax (if in the Syntax Editor), and so forth.

# Data Transformations

All of the examples in this manual assume that all of your data have been entered into SPSS in ready-to-use form. There are many situations, however, in which you might wish to create new variables from existing ones, or change the values of existing variables after the data have been entered. SPSS for Windows offers a variety of options for transforming data in these ways. In this appendix we briefly describe a few of the most commonly used ones.

## Computing a New Variable

One kind of data transformation involves creating a new variable based on a mathematical formula involving your original variables. For example, your data might include responses to five questionnaire items that you wish to add up to construct a "total" score. Although you could do these computations yourself and then enter the *total* variable into the Data Editor, there are many advantages to entering the original five variables into the Data Editor and then letting SPSS create the *total* variable for you. Not only is this likely to be faster, but SPSS won't make any arithmetic errors.

Suppose you have entered into the Data Editor scores on five variables for each of your subjects, and named the variables *q1*, *q2*, and so forth. Now you want to create a new variable named *total*, which, for each subject, represents the sum of his or her responses to the five questions. You can use either the Point-and-Click Method or the Syntax Method to compute a new variable using virtually any mathematical equation you can imagine.

*Conditional Computations.* Sometimes you want to compute a new variable (1) for only certain subjects or (2) by using a different formula for different subjects, depending on the subjects' scores on other variable(s). Such "conditional computations" are also easy to do using either method.

### Point-and-Click Method

After entering your data into the Data Editor, click on **Transform** on the menu bar, and then choose **Compute Variable . . . .** This produces a large dialog box (see Figure B.1) that contains a list of your variables (for this example **q1**, **q2**, and so on) on the left; blank sections labeled "Target Variable" and "Numeric Expression" at the top; and a section resembling a calculator in the middle.

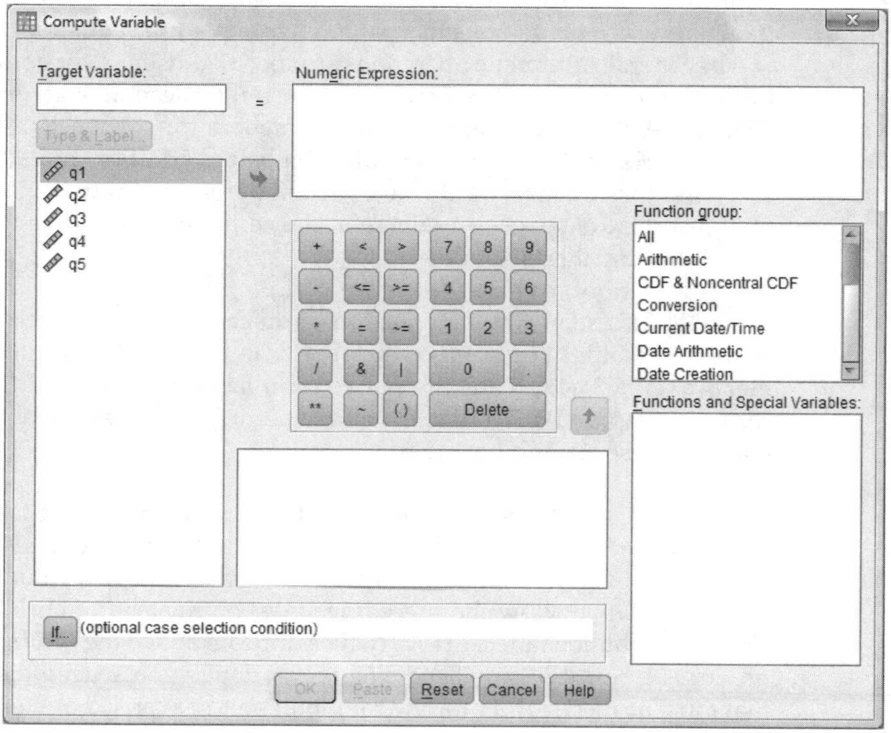

**Figure B.1**

To create the new variable, first click in the box labeled "Target Variable" and type the word **total** (or whatever you wish to name the new variable). Then click in the box to the right labeled "Numeric Expression," and type an algebraic formula indicating how this variable is to be computed. For this example, you would type **q1 + q2 + q3 + q4 + q5**. (Alternatively, you might want to compute the new variable as the average of the five variables rather than the sum by typing **(q1 + q2 + q3 + q4 + q5) / 5**.) After typing the desired equation, click on **OK** and you're done. If you go back and look at the Data Editor, you'll see that a new column called "total" has been added at the end. You might want to compute a few *total* scores by hand to confirm SPSS's computations.

Another way to construct your equation is by selecting (by clicking on) the equation components, one by one, from the various parts of the window. For example, after typing **total** into the "Target Variable" box, you can create your equation by first clicking on **q1** in the variable list on the left; then, click on the arrow button next to this list and **q1** will appear in the "Numeric Expression" box as if you had just typed it yourself. Next, click on **+** in the calculator section of the window, and **+** appears after **q1** in the "Numeric Expression" box. You can construct the entire equation this way, step by step, though this is more tedious than simply typing out the equation.

In general, arithmetic operations are specified using **+** for addition (as in the example above), **-** for subtraction, **\*** for multiplication, and **/** for division. SPSS understands the standard rules of algebra for sequence of operations (for example, multiplication and division before addition and subtraction), and parentheses can be used where needed or for clarification. Note that you may insert extra spaces anywhere in the command (as above) to enhance readability, but this is not necessary.

In addition, a variety of more complex mathematical functions is available for use in writing equations. You can find them listed in the box under the words "Function group." For example, **sum(q1,q2,q3,q4,q5)** and **mean(q1,q2,q3,q4,q5)** are alternative formulas for the *total* variable in our earlier examples. With a little experimentation you should be able to figure many of these out and how to use them.

*Conditional Computations.*   Suppose that you have another variable in your data set called *group*, and you want to compute *total* as described above only for subjects in group 1 (that is, only for subjects who have a value of 1 on the variable *group*). Follow the preceding steps, but instead of clicking on **OK**, click on the button labeled **If . . .** (which appears above the **OK** button). This produces a new (but similar) dialog box in which you specify the condition that must be met in order for the computation to be carried out. First, click in the little circle next to the phrase "Include if case satisfies condition." Then click in the box directly below this phrase, and type an equation specifying the selection criterion. In this case, the formula is simply **group = 1**. Now click on **Continue** to return to the main "Compute Variable" dialog box, and then click on **OK** to execute the instructions. If you were to go back to the Data Editor, you would see that the new variable *total* appears in the last column, but only some of your subjects (those in group 1) have a value on this variable. All others simply have a dot (indicating a "missing value") for the variable *total*.

Alternatively, use any of the following in place of the equals sign within parentheses: **<** or **LT** for "less than," **>** or **GT** for "greater than," **<=** or **LE** for "less than or equal to," or **>=** or **GE** for "greater than or equal to." **EQ** can also be used in place of **=**.

If you wish, you can now compute values for *total* for other subjects using an alternative formula. For example, *total* may be computed as the sum of questions 6 through 10 (instead of 1 through 5) for subjects in group 2. Simply follow the steps just described, substituting the new expressions as appropriate. When you click on **OK**, SPSS will present a pop-up warning box asking if you want to "Change existing variable?" This is because the variable you are creating (*total*) already exists—you created it in the previous step when computing scores for group 1. Now you are modifying an existing variable rather than creating a new one; you are changing "missing" scores for group

2 subjects (which is what they were after the first step) to the computed values you want. So, simply click **OK.** It is still a good idea, however, to pause for a moment to make sure you haven't made a mistake. It is always dangerous to change the values of an existing variable because, in some cases, it is difficult to undo the change if you later realize you made an error.

Syntax Method

After you enter data into the Data Editor, open the Syntax Editor and type a single command, beginning with the word **COMPUTE,** and specify the equation for creating the new variable. For example, the command

```
COMPUTE TOTAL = Q1 + Q2 + Q3 + Q4 + Q5.
```

creates a new variable called **TOTAL,** which, for each subject, is assigned a value equal to the sum of the variables **Q1, Q2, . . . , Q5**. Alternatively, you might want to compute the new variable as an average rather than a sum; in this case type

```
COMPUTE TOTAL = (Q1 + Q2 + Q3 + Q4 + Q5) / 5.
```

Whichever you choose, type the command exactly as you see it written (don't forget the period at the end!) and run it by following the procedures explained in Chapter 4. If you were to go back and look at the Data Editor, you would see that a new column called "total" has been added at the end. You might want to compute a few *total* scores by hand to confirm SPSS's values.

You can specify virtually any kind of algebraic equation on a **COMPUTE** command to create a new variable as a function of existing variables. You always specify the name of the new variable first, followed by an equal sign, followed by an algebraic expression. Arithmetic operations are specified using + for addition, - for subtraction, * for multiplication, and / for division. SPSS understands the standard rules for sequence of operations (for example, multiplication and division before addition and subtraction), and parentheses can be used where needed or just to make things clear. Note that you may insert extra spaces anywhere in the command to enhance readability, but this is not necessary.

In addition, a variety of more complex mathematical functions is available for use in writing equations. For example, **SUM(Q1,Q2,Q3,Q4,Q5)** and **MEAN(Q1,Q2,Q3,Q4,Q5)** are alternative formulas for the *total* variable in our examples above. You can find a list of these options in the dialog box as described in the preceding *Point-and-Click Method* section.

*Conditional Computations.*   Suppose that you have another variable in your data set called *group,* and you want to compute *total* as described above only for subjects in group 1 (that is, only for subjects who have a value of 1 on the variable *group*). This is accomplished by using a different command,

**IF**, instead of **COMPUTE**. In the present example, type this command into the Syntax Editor:

```
IF (GROUP = 1) TOTAL = Q1 + Q2 + Q3 + Q4 + Q5.
```

You have simply replaced the word **COMPUTE** with the word **IF**, followed by an equation in parentheses that describes the condition under which the computation is to be carried out. In this example, TOTAL will be computed by summing the variables **Q1** through **Q5**, but only for those subjects for whom the variable **GROUP** has a value of 1. If you were to go back to the Data Editor, you would see that the new variable *total* appears in the last column, and only some of your subjects (those in group 1) have a value on this variable. All others simply have a dot (indicating a "missing value") on *total*.

Alternatively, use any of the following in place of the equals sign within parentheses: **<** or **LT** for "less than," **>** or **GT** for "greater than," **<=** or **LE** for "less than or equal to," or **>=** or **GE** for "greater than or equal to." **EQ** can also be used in place of **=**.

If you wish, you can now compute values for *total* for your other subjects using some other formula. For example, *total* might be computed as the sum of questions 6 through 10 (instead of 1 through 5) for subjects in group 2. To accomplish this, simply type a second command after the command above specifying these instructions. For example, the second command might be

```
IF (GROUP = 2) TOTAL = Q6 + Q7 + Q8 + Q9 + Q10.
```

It is worth noting that when SPSS executes the first of these **IF** commands, it is creating a new variable called *total*; however, when it then executes the second command, the variable *total* already exists (by virtue of the first command). It is therefore not creating a new variable, but instead modifying an existing one. You are changing "missing" scores for group 2 subjects (which is what they were after the first step) to the computed values you want.

## Recoding Values of an Existing Variable

Another common data transformation involves changing the numerical codes assigned to different values of a variable, a process called *recoding* a variable. For example, suppose you had entered the data for the variable *sex* with 1's for men and 0's for women, and then later for some reason decided that you instead wanted to use 2's for men and 1's for women. Once the data have been entered into the Data Editor, you can use either the Point-and-Click Method or the Syntax Method to switch these values, or to change some or all of the values to entirely new values (for example, change all the 0's to 7's and all the 1's to 28's).

*Creating a New Variable.*    It is dangerous to alter the data for an existing variable. If you make a mistake, it might be difficult to undo the change and correct the original data. Both the Point-and-Click Method and the Syntax Method make it easy to save the results of the recoding as a new variable with its own name, leaving the original variable unchanged. We generally recommend this procedure to be on the safe side.

### Point-and-Click Method

After you enter your data into the Data Editor, click on **Transform** on the menu bar, and then choose **Recode**. This will produce another small menu. Choose **Into Same Variables . . . .** The resulting dialog box, shown in Figure B.2, contains a list of your variables on the left. Move the variable(s) you want to recode from the left box to the right box (labeled "Variables"), and then click on **Old and New Values . . . .**

In the next dialog box there are several ways to specify the recoding; we discuss the simplest one here. In the left column under "Old Value" and next to the word "Value," type the first value of the variable you wish to change. If, as in our previous example, you wanted to change all the 0's to 1's, type **0** in this box. Then click in the box to the right, under "New Value," and type the value you want—in this case **1**. Next, click on the button labeled **Add**, just below your new value. A box in the lower right of the screen shows the results of your transformation. It now says "0 -> 1." The other boxes will be blank, and you can repeat the steps for any other values you wish to recode. To complete this example, type **1** in the "Old Value" box and **2** in the "New

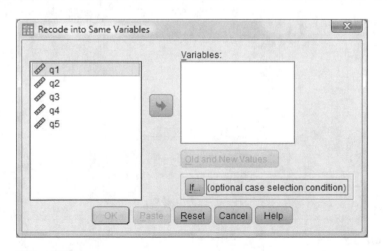

**Figure B.2**

Value" box, then click on **Add** again, and finally click on **Continue** when you're done. At the main "Recode" dialog box, click on **OK** to execute the changes. The data in the Data Editor are now changed accordingly and will appear just as if you had originally entered 1's and 2's.

*Creating a New Variable.*    We recommend that you save the modified variable under a new name and leave the original variable unchanged. First, choose **Recode** from the menu bar (as before), but then choose **Into Different Variables . . .** from the next menu. This brings up a dialog box, shown in Figure B.3, that is similar to the one discussed in the preceding section, but with one extra feature. Choose the variable you wish to recode from the list in the left-hand box, and move it to the right-hand box. Now, however, you must specify the name of the new variable you wish to create (that will contain the modified values). On the right side of the dialog box, under "Output Variable," there is a small box labeled "Name"; click in this box and type the name of the new variable you wish to create. In this example, you might call the modified variable **sex2**. Then click on **Old and New Values . . .** , and follow the remainder of the procedure just described. A new variable with the specified name (*sex2*) will be created (and can be seen in the Data Editor), in which the men have 2's and the women have 1's. The original *sex* variable will still be there, unchanged, and both variables are now available for use in future analyses.

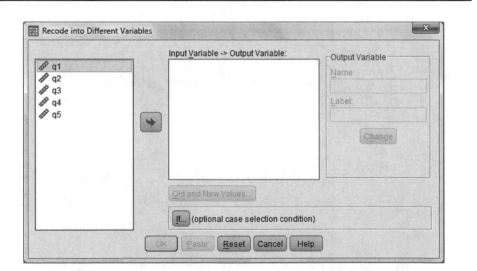

**Figure B.3**

Syntax Method

In the Syntax Editor, you can recode by typing and running a **RECODE** command. A **RECODE** command consists of the word **RECODE** followed immediately by the name(s) of one or more variables whose values you wish to change and one or more parenthetical expressions indicating the desired numerical changes. Each set of parentheses specifies a "from" value and a "to" value separated by an equals sign. For example, the command

```
RECODE SEX (0=1)(1=2).
```

tells SPSS to change, on the variable *sex*, all of the 0's to 1's and all of the 1's to 2's. (Think of the equals signs as right-pointing arrows.) After executing this command, the data in the Data Editor are changed accordingly and appear just as if you had initially entered 1's and 2's. You may include as many sets of parentheses as needed; it is permissible to have multiple "from" values re-coded into the same "to" value—for example, **(1=0)(2=0)(3=0)** would change 1's, 2's, and 3's to 0's (zeros). Alternatively, you can accomplish all of this within one set of parentheses by typing **(1,2,3=0)**.

*Creating a New Variable.*    We recommend that you save the modified variable under a new name and leave the original variable unchanged. Simply alter the **RECODE** command by adding the phrase **INTO NEWNAME** (where *newname* is the name you want to give the newly created variable) to the end of the command, after the parenthetical statements. For example, the preceding command can be written

```
RECODE SEX (0=1)(1=2) INTO SEX2.
```

A new variable with the specified name (*sex2*) will be created (and can be seen in the Data Editor), in which the men have 2's and the women have 1's. The original *sex* variable will still be there, unchanged, and both variables are now available for use in future analyses.

## Selecting Cases for Analysis

This section explains briefly how to select a subset of your subjects for inclu-sion in one or more analyses. For example, you might want to compute a set of correlations among several variables, but you want to do so separately for men and for women. If you have a variable (for example, *sex*) in your data set to define the subgroup of interest, this is easy to accomplish without actually having to delete unwanted cases from your data.

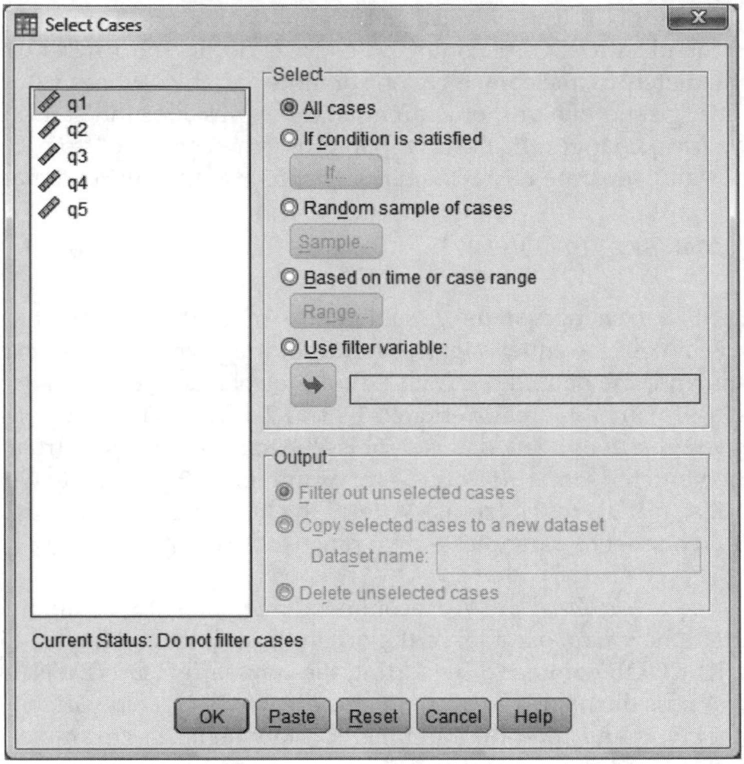

**Figure B.4**

Point-and-Click Method

From the menu bar, click on **Data** and choose **Select Cases** . . . in the pull-down menu. This produces a dialog box (see Figure B.4) containing a list of your variables on the left and several options from which to choose on the right. In the list on the right, notice that "All cases" is selected. Click on the circle to the left of "If condition is satisfied," and then click on the **If** . . . button below. This opens a new dialog box similar to the one described earlier in this appendix, in the section *Conditional Computations* on page 108. In the upper-right box, type an equation representing the condition that must be met for a subject to be included in subsequent analyses. For example, type **sex = 1** to select only men (if men have a value of 1 on the variable *sex*), or type **total < 15** to select only individuals whose score on the variable *total* is less than 15. (See the section entitled *Conditional Computations* on page 108 for more details on specifying conditions.) Then click on **Continue** to return to the main "Select Cases" dialog box, and click on **OK** to put the selection criterion into operation. Any analyses specified subsequently will include only those subjects who have been selected.

If, later in your SPSS session, you wish to conduct analyses including all of your subjects, you can turn off the selection criterion by again choosing **Data**, then **Select Cases . . .** , from the menu bar, then choose "All cases" in the dialog box.

Syntax Method

Open the Syntax Editor and type a command that begins with **SELECT IF** and is followed by an equation in parentheses specifying the selection criterion. For example,

```
SELECT IF (SEX = 1).
```

tells SPSS to select from the data set only those subjects having a value of 1 on the variable *sex*. The rules for specifying conditions within parentheses are the same as for the **IF** command described earlier in this appendix (see the section *Conditional Computations* on page 108 for more details).

Once a **SELECT IF** command is executed, it remains in effect for the remainder of that SPSS session. That is, if you execute the preceding command, all subsequent commands and procedures will be restricted to subjects for whom the variable *sex* equals 1. (*Note:* If you do this, be sure not to resave your data file with the same name, or you will permanently lose the unselected cases!)

If you wish to *temporarily* select a subset of cases for just a single analysis or procedure, you must precede your **SELECT IF** command with the simple command **TEMPORARY**, as follows:

```
TEMPORARY.
SELECT IF (SEX = 1).
```

"Temporary" in this case means, "only for the next statistical analysis conducted." That is, if the next command you execute is, say, a **CORRELATIONS** or a **T-TEST** command, that particular analysis will be restricted to subjects with *sex* equal to 1. After the analysis is finished, all cases are then restored for any subsequent analyses unless you execute another **SELECT IF** command.